Joys of Self-Determined Learning: A Collection of Essays

By Carlo Ricci and Gina Riley

Editor Biographies:

Carlo Ricci is a full Professor at the Schulich School of Education, Nipissing University, Graduate Studies. He founded and edits the *Journal of Unschooling and Alternative Learning* (*JUAL*). He has published a number of books and articles. His research interests include unschooling; homeschooling; holistic education; self-determined learning; free schools; democratic schools; online learning; technology and learning; play; natural learning; curiosity; willed learning; the willed curriculum; critical pedagogy; and healthy living.

Gina Riley is a Clinical Professor and Program Leader of the Adolescent Special Education Program at City University of New York, Hunter College. Dr. Riley has over twenty-five years of experience in online education and distance learning at the college/university level. She is known internationally for her work in the fields of homeschooling, unschooling, and self-directed learning. Her books include *Unschooling: Exploring Learning Beyond The Classroom* (Palgrave Macmillan, 2020) and *The Homeschooling Starter Guide* (Rockridge Press, 2021).

Table of Contents

Carlo Ricci and Gina Riley

Introduction

Carlo Ricci & Gina Riley

At its most basic this book is about learning. More specifically about whether it is possible to empower the learner? We are happy to write that, based on the narratives shared throughout this book, the answer is a resounding yes. The narratives throughout this book show that people can learn and still be empowered, free, and self-determined.

Self-Determined versus Self-Directed

Throughout this book many of the authors use the word self-directed, but we prefer to use the word self-determined or willed learning. Although, it would be fair to say that within this book we are all using self-determined and self-directed interchangeably, we still prefer self-determined because we believe that self-directed has been co-opted by mainstream schooling. When mainstream schooling uses the term self-directed they mean something very different than we do by it. What they mean is that they tell the learner what to learn, and then the learners go ahead and learn it in the way that makes sense to them, within reason, which means within what those in power sanction and allow. Self-determined can also mean intrinsically motivated, which is what all self-directed learning really is, coming from one's strengths, interests, and passions. So, we are using self-determined in the introduction in an attempt to avoid confusion between self-directed as the authors use it in

Introduction

this book and how we understand it, with how
mainstream schoolers use it. If it's easier, we suggest
that when you read self-directed throughout this book
feel free to substitute it with self-determined or willed
learning, which is where the learner gets to decide what
to learn, when, where, how, and why to learn.

Learning and Empowerment

One powerful revelation that the narratives
within this book elucidates is that learning can happen if
the learner is empowered and decides what to learn,
when, where, how, and why to learn. None of this is a
surprise to those of us who have been championing self-
determined approaches and bearing witness firsthand to
the power of willed learning. There is no doubt that an
empowered person can learn without the presence of
coercion.

Control versus Liberation

Some self-determined learning advocates believe
that since its inception schooling was designed to control
people's minds, bodies, spirits, and emotions.
Mainstream schools were never meant to be about
freedom and liberation, and have always been about
control and coercion. So, it's expected for mainstream
schooling to be set up the way that it is. It's expected
that learners' minds, bodies, spirits, and emotions are
being controlled, since that's what mainstream schooling
is meant to do and, accordingly, that is what it does.

Just because that is what mainstream schooling was designed to do, does not mean that in our contemporary world that that is what it should continue to do. Many of us believe, and hopefully many more will agree, that learning should be about love, peace, respect, care, compassion, trust, freedom, democracy and so on. Learning can and should be done willingly and gently, and not forcefully, and without internal motivation. In fact, we believe that when learning is done with all of the above in mind, that that is when it can be most powerful. In short, willed learning is ethically and substantively better than forced learning, especially if we are interested in democracy.

Unfortunately, mainstream schooling is not done freely and lovingly, and so, shamefully, we sometimes end up with awful realities. For example, during the school year, some students take more prescription medications, check themselves into hospitals, commit suicide, and report being frequently stressed. Traditional schooling can be physically, emotionally and socially hurtful, instead of the helpful place it was intended to be. In a recent podcast hosted by Adrian Cheung (2020, August 12), Dr. Tyler Black, child and adolescent psychiatrist at the University of British Columbia stated:

> My job is easier during summer and non-school days because kids are less in crisis. I see less kids and my primary research interest being suicide, we know for certain that the highest rates of suicide are during school months and school days for kids.

Introduction

This shocking reality needs to stop, and we hope that the narratives in this book will help shed light on what others are already doing to reveal what loving, healing and self-determined possibilities exist.

What to Learn

Mainstream schooling is designed to train people to be compliant. What to learn is dictated and forced on students from an external source, and often grades are used as punishment and rewards to make sure that students comply and are controlled. The student has little or no choice in the curriculum. Whether they are interested or not is of little consequence. They are told what to learn and they have to comply or face the consequences. Schools act as gatekeepers and if students refuse, the gate may be shut. In this sense, schools may not create opportunities for people, but they actually limit what options people have. Of course, there are always backdoors (for example, open universities) that people can access if they know how to access them and know that they exist.

Fortunately, this is not the only way. As the learning approaches outlined in this book make clear, people can be trusted and respected to learn what they are interested in. People can create their personal curriculum or they can learn as they live their lives. The best definition for learning comes from John Holt. Holt (1989) writes, "Living is learning. It is impossible to be alive and conscious (and some would say unconscious) without constantly learning things" (p. 157). So, whether the student creates their own curriculum or it emerges

Carlo Ricci and Gina Riley

organically, the approaches outlined in this book differ significantly from mainstream schools, even in the most progressive sense of mainstream schooling.

When to Learn

Mainstream schools also dictate when children have to learn. There is a set time for students to learn and often if assignments are not completed on time students are punished, and if they are completed on time and they are done consistent with what is ordered, they are rewarded. Students have to learn on command and they are even timed during tests, for example, to make sure that they learn when expected. In a democracy this is very frightening and inconsistent with the ideals of freedom, decency, and dignity.

In contrast, the narratives shared in this book offer a different way. Learning can (and does) happen at any time. Sometimes the learner consciously wills to learn something, and in others it simply happens organically. Either way, the learning becomes intrinsically motivated, self-determined, and based on the individual's strengths, interests, and wishes. This type of learning also allows for more integration, generalization, and reflection.

Where to Learn

Mainstream schools are set up to have people learn mostly within institutions. Some schools were purposefully built without windows so that the learners would not be distracted by anything outside of the room.

Introduction

Even virtual classrooms often have technology built in so that the learner is focused on what is happening within the virtual classroom and is not "distracted" by other things.

Again, in contrast, the approaches within this book understand that learning can happen anywhere and at any time. They do not place a hierarchy on learning and are respectful and allow the learners to learn wherever they want, and wherever it makes most sense. Learners are not forced to be there whether it makes sense or not, but instead they can go to where the learner feels they need to be and where it makes most sense to be.

How to Learn

Mainstream schooling dictates how students need to learn. They often provide assignments with specific instructions that dictate how students need to learn. Rubrics are often used as a method of grading and a technology of control and tests are given to assess learning. Most administrators may not really care how deeply students learn or absorb material. Instead, they are focused on the grade a student gets or the percentage a student achieves, because that is what they are taught to focus on.

The approaches in this book once again replace this rigid model with one that is more freeing. The learners themselves are the ones who self-determine how (and if) they want to learn one thing or another. The adults become facilitators, instead of the leaders, of the learning process.

Carlo Ricci and Gina Riley

Why to Learn

Often, we hear mainstream schoolers ask the question, "why do we need to learn this?" Teachers often make up a response that is often insufficient or plainly misguided. We are not being facetious, but we cannot think of anything that every single person needs to learn, and especially at the same time. This makes absolutely no sense, especially if we respect the diversity of the human experience. Sometimes the explanation for why they need to learn one thing or another is externally motivated. They need to learn it so that they can then go on to more schooling, for instance; or they need to learn it so they can pass a state mandated exam.

Mercifully, the approaches highlighted in this book leave it to the learner to respond which leads to them being internally motivated to learn one thing or another. They are not forced or coerced to learn and so if they do not have a reason that makes sense to them, then they can move on to something that does. The power lies with them and they are the ones who are empowered.

How the Book is Divided

Part 1 of the book focuses on individuals who have been part of the self-determined learning movement. Some are homeschooling, unschooling, or worldschooling parents, others have created their own self-directed learning centers or environments. Part 1 includes essays from unschooling greats such as Akilah Richard and Dr. Rebecca English. Robin Alpern's essay

Introduction

"The School of Benign Neglect" is particularly facetious, as Robin is obviously a caring, thoughtful mother who paid particular attention not only to her children, but to the homeschooling group she co-founded, making sure all children had the opportunity to deeply learn through a myriad of activities.

Part 1 also includes essays by Project World School founder Lainie Liberti, and worldschooler Dr. Kate Green. Incredible narratives of self-determined learning also came from the Directors and Facilitators of Self-Directed Learning Centers across the United States and Canada. Writers of these narratives include Ken Danford of North Star, Katy Burke of Princeton Learning Cooperative, Carol Nash of Alpha II, Maysaa Bazna of Pono in New York City, and Hope Wilder of Pathfinder Learning Center in North Carolina.

Part 2 is focused on those who have been exposed to self-directed learning throughout their lives. Writer and blogger Idzie Desmaris starts off the section with a brilliant piece about growing up unschooled. Sulaf Hatab enthusiastically shares what it is like to learn within the self-directed center her mother, Maysaa Banza, founded. Miro Siegal writes beautifully about growing up worldschooled. Jasmine Higgins, A.S. Neill's great granddaughter, gives a fantastic account of her experience at Summerhill.

Conclusion

As you can see by these essays, in each one, the learner is free and can self-determine and fully control what, when, where, how, and why they learn. The clear

xiii

advantage of this is that it respects the child or teen and it is ethically the right thing to do. We are all different and we have different strengths, weaknesses, and interests. The approaches in this book allow people to unfold in ways that make most sense to them. It permits them to maximize all of the learning that actually exists in the world, since they are not limited and forced to learn what others impose on them. They can formally choose and learn absolutely anything, or they can simply be and learn to be mindful and absorb the world around them as they live their lives.

Finally, the many worldviews illustrated in this book offer a variety of responses to the question "what is the purpose of learning?" What all of the essays illustrate is that learning is meant to prepare people to participate in the world we live in. All of this coupled with the fact that there is no critical period to learn any academic subjects, makes the approaches in this book perfect for a free and loving democratic world.

References

Cheung, A. (Host). (2020, August 12). Schools are the best place for kids' mental health? Not so fast [Audio podcast episode]. In *The Toronto Star*. This Matters. https://www.thestar.com/podcasts/thismatters/2020/08/12/schools-are-the-best-place-for-kids-mental-health-not-so-fast.html

Holt, J. (1989). *Learning all the time: How small children begin to read, write, count,*

and investigate the world, without being taught.
USA: Da Cappo Books.

Part 1: What is Self-Determined Learning?

Chapter 1

Rhythms & Realizations in Unschooling: How Learning is Personal For Each of Us

Akilah Richards

"Everything in the universe has a **rhythm**, everything dances."—Maya Angelou

Much of my life is spent observing and remembering how to honor rhythm; not just my own, but the rhythm inherent in all things, and my children are part of all things. The design of our days as a family isn't at all about a particular structure or even a particular interest. Instead, it is rhythmic, and it is informed largely by each of our desires to feel unobstructed in our walk toward joy and fulfillment. We experience learning as an inside thing, an outside thing, and a bit of everything. It doesn't exist inside a book or a person, but books, people, and other resources sometimes embody vibrations that go really well with our intrinsic rhythm. For me specifically, this noticing and deliberateness around rhythm, though a mainstay in my life for as long as I remember, is far more consistent since I began the practice of unschooling. Through my *Rhythm Studies*, my approach to learning continues to expand and slow down, leaving me plenty of space to see learning as an ever-present element of being alive, and as something I tap into consciously and unconsciously, through tangible things and things only felt through emotions, to any and everything in between. My best spaces for observation so far have been through Marley and Sage, who are also Kris's and my daughters.

Akilah Richards

They were our first big disruption from standardized education, so I thought it useful to share our daughters' approaches to learning. As I continue this slow shedding of the schoolishness that taught me that learning was about displaying *knowledge*, I am constantly in awe of the ways that Marley and Sage take ownership of their learning. Though the four of us—my daughters, Kris, and me—all identify as unschoolers, most certainly, the ways we unschool differ and are deeply personal for each of us. I still navigate the schoolish need to show what I've learned, or to low-key *prove* that what I'm doing is working, and I really appreciate observing that Marley and Sage don't have that ailment. They don't seem to feel the need to *show* that they've learned something. Instead, their knowledge shows up in our conversations, activities, and everyday life experiences with our daughters, and through experiences relayed to us by other people with whom our girls spend time.

"It's a pretty tight process, just never done in a timely manner."

That's Sage's response to my question to her about her approach to learning, and I love how she immediately speaks to the slow pace of her process. Sage is, at the time I'm writing this, 14-years-old. She was in public school for less than two years (ages six and seven), and spent a year (at age 12) at a self-directed learning space (Heartwood Agile Learning Center) in Atlanta. Mostly though, since she was about seven-years-old, she has been part of our location-independent, unschooling family, learning through life experiences and sporadic formal lessons, as she (rarely) chooses, mostly online.

> My approach to learning is basically to collect stuff and roll with it. So, I do a lot of research around a topic and if something about the research is interesting, then I shift from broader research to a specific set of rabbit holes, which usually gets me to what I want, which usually turns out to be a specific aspect of the big, broad thing I was researching. (S. Richards, personal communication, August 20, 2020)

I asked her if she could think of a recent time when she applied her process and got what she wanted. She immediately recalled how comic books helped her define the styles of art and writing that she most enjoyed and wanted to practice. The impetus was her not feeling clear about the "genres or vibes of art" that she liked most, and wanting to have a different feeling. She started by focusing on the types of stories she wanted to read, particularly with comic books, then zoomed in on the art styles within them. She researched and read tons of comic books, which led to some interesting and obscure comic book findings, particularly in the manga genre. Through researching and then going down a rabbit hole with mostly obscure manga, she discovered artists whose styles she enjoyed, but unexpectedly, started finding writers whose styles she enjoyed as well. Her end goal was achieved, which was to find clarity around the vibe/style of art she likes, which turns out to go beyond genre. The bonus knowledge came in the form of new writing inspiration and interests. Now, Sage sees this process as *hers*, one she intuited, and one she says she effectively applies to just about anything she wants to find out or get into. As we talked about her process, we synthesized it as a four-part thing:

1.   Name
2.   Research
3.   Rabbit Hole
4.   Result

Here's how she describes her process, in her own words:

> The goal here is to find a name for what I'm looking for. I wondered how one would go about finding a name for a thing online. Like, if I don't know what it is, how would I research it? [Sage's response is so interesting!]
>
> Because I do so much general research, I tend to know a lot of words that speak generally to what I'm looking for. For example, all my researching has led me to be able to gauge the general region that a language is from—language groups, basically, which is helpful when trying to find the origin or the spin-off of something. So, for example, if I hear about something and want to research it, I can say, based on what I know, that's a Germanic language (German, Dutch, Flemish, Luxembourgish, etc.), and I can add related keywords to drill down the focus.

> Relating an idea to things in my brain (like language groups) helps me to narrow it down pretty organically, because some things will clash, you know, they just won't fit. For example, something couldn't be both Germanic and Asian (though Asian isn't a language group, the sound is distinctively different, so it helps to narrow the focus), so I'd go with the one that actually matches whatever I do know, which helps me get closer to what I don't yet know. What I'm searching for may be as broad as a category or as narrow as a title, but it's usually enough to start searching, and from there, I narrow down and move to the next step, which is research. (S. Richards, personal communication, August 20, 2020)

Research: Then it goes from broad (naming) to more specific research, and it becomes "an elimination process" to get her to her rabbit holes, where the deep dive begins.

Rabbit hole: Sage says,

> I tend to take notes at this phase because I'm always going to come across words that I'm not familiar with, and since my computer is slow, I can't risk wasting time looking up a word a bunch of different times because I forgot I already looked it up (it being new to me and all). So, I take notes of words/findings that are new so I don't click on them over and over. Also, music

is pretty important at this stage because I'm doing a lot of skimming and discarding, and music helps me get into a good space with that. The skimming is great, it's the most fun part of the process for me because it doesn't call for a deep focus, the way the first part does, and I get to look at a lot of new images and apply what I'm finding to my original research. Plus, skimming is what broadens my base knowledge; it's how I know a lot of things about a lot of different topics, and I like that feeling. (S. Richards, personal communication, August 20, 2020)

Result: "I end up with answers for what I was originally searching for, and a broadening of my base knowledge."

I've seen Sage work through this process to figure out what aspects of a thing actually interest her, like going from liking a piece of art in a museum, to realizing that she actually only liked the texture of the piece, then finding out it was needlework, and then diving into needlework, asking me to take her to the needlework circle at a nearby library, and then meeting people who do specific types of needlework. Those particular spaces tend to be comprised mostly of women elders, which is so wonderful to experience the intergenerational learning and friendliness, all of which are part of her learning experience, not just the needlework itself. The conversations I've heard her have with women in their seventies and eighties who could tell her more than just details about their needlework processes, but about the history of a thing, and the evolution of it over time in certain places. Those gems heightened her interests and often complements her steady interests in history and culture. Nothing happens in a vacuum, and self-directedness/determination feels to me, to be inextricably linked to a pattern of new discoveries and expanded interests, with personal processes for mining and using the new information.

Marley is 16-years-old at this moment, and like Sage, spends most of her time in independent exploration, meaning we aren't connected to a particular self-directed center or group, outside of the year they both spent at Heartwood. She also has a longstanding interest in languages and the details therein, and when I asked her about her approach to learning, I wasn't surprised to hear that her language studies significantly inform her approach to, and experiences with learning.

> How I approach deliberately trying to *learn* something depends on the level of proficiency I want to reach with that specific thing. So, the approach that I took to learning Japanese, because I wanted to be fluent in it, was a very different approach than the one I took to learning coding because I was only passively interested. When I started learning to code, I was really just drilling the basics. My plan was to find a really simple course and just take that, which I did. Whereas my Japanese [learning] plan was more of a long game, so I looked into tutors, I looked into workbooks, language partners, language apps, all sorts of things before I even really officially got started with the mindset that it was more than a passing interest. It became an official

pursuit, I guess, for the same reasons I end up taking a deeper interest in some other things—it's because I feel something is missing from my initial experience with the thing. Specifically, with Japanese, it was because I was watching anime I really enjoyed and found out that the subtitles were done by a native English speaker, not a native Japanese speaker. I was about nine [years old] and I remember being so upset! I was so sure that I was missing out on the real feelings and intentions behind the story, so I stopped watching anime with English sub[title]s and just listened to them. I also started watching music videos in Japanese and listening to music, and my interest grew. When I first started learning Japanese, I was way too much in my head, so over time, the long-game approach I mentioned was developed to help me fix that feeling of being stuck in my head with the concept of Japanese [language]. I realized that planning ahead, you know, looking for resources around the language and planning how to engage them, is what I found to be much more helpful. Once I have a trajectory, then I pretty much take things by weekly progress or monthly progress. I started out doing daily progress check-ins but quickly learned that that doesn't work for me; it feels like I'm not really getting anything done, so I take things by the week, or even the month, so I can see my own progress over an extended time. (M. Richards, personal communication, August 20, 2020)

Chapter 1

I asked Marley whether she felt or feels equipped to gauge her own progress in a language that isn't native to her, or anything that was new to her, for that matter. She said yes, and then went on to talk about why and how.

> I, personally, use some kind of test at the end of each section of learning to gauge my proficiency because the way that I learn anything now was shaped by how I learned language, and when you're learning a language you need to constantly be drilling the past thing and building on top of it. So, if you move on to week three, then you need to look at week two's content again, while moving on to week four, that kind of thing. That was something that came to me kind of naturally. I just noticed that, if I wasn't consistent and practicing the whole skill, but only specific sections, then it wouldn't work. So, if I was only practicing grammar at the time, then I would notice that my vocabulary [skill level] would fall significantly. Turns out I have to practice them all in conjunction and I think that's an important thing for me anyway; an important part of learning is doing everything together so that the full picture is apparent to me, and I can work from there. (M. Richards, personal communication, August 20, 2020)

I asked Marley whether she thought this approach might be specific to language studies, and whether she had taken that approach and applied it to anything else. She brought up her experience starting a podcast and organizing a production team.

> I had a podcast on *Rwby Amino* for a few months. It was during a time that we were traveling to places with different time zones, and I realized that I needed to plan if I was going to publish consistently. So, I had a whole plan. I wrote out my interview questions, I identified the weeks that I was available to do interviews, which were times that we weren't traveling or scheduled to go somewhere in our new city. I set up all of my time around taking in those interviews, and spent a couple of days before that writing detailed scripts for the first three episodes. While I was interviewing, I was also writing up related intake forms. During the first couple of episodes we had a section dedicated to shouting out smaller creators, for example, so I was drafting things and speaking with other artists at the same time that I was interviewing people. Again, I was working with all the pieces so that everything would work for the first few episodes, and everything would run smoothly. (M. Richards, personal communication, August 20, 2020)

I asked her if she had done any research around the process of putting a podcast together.

> No, I didn't even start calling it a podcast until very recently. All I understood when I started *Rwby Radio* was that I want to talk about

particular things with other people. And I want other people to hear them, because, again, that felt missing from my experience as a *Rwby* fan because most of what I saw were writing-based discussion boards. So, I was like, okay what resources are available for me to use in a way that's easier for me? And the answer to that was using the video screening room [inside *Rwby Amino*]. From there, I thought, okay well if it was just me in the room it would look kind of strange so then I guess I need to have someone do some good-looking cover art for me. From there, I started to build a team based on the things that would make it stand out. So, I just thought of things as they went along and as the needs showed up. Actually, within the first couple of weeks, one or two of the positions that I had originally put out, I ended up not needing, or I realized I didn't ever actually need. Over time I saw things that could be delegated to somebody else besides me, and other things that weren't necessary at all, like understudies for the co-host and all that. So, there were a lot of little parts that I just took out as the months went on; trial and error, testing out based on what made sense for me at the time, and then pivoting where needed. It was super intuitive. (M. Richards, personal communication, August 20, 2020)

I wondered and asked if she felt any fear at any point. Particularly fear around not having a set plan and leaving it to "chance" instead of having it planned out section by section, and risking something going horribly wrong.

> I was never concerned with the lack of conventional planning, because I had had previous projects where I didn't plan, I just moved with a framework in mind, and that works for me. I even ended up writing my first article back then, "How to Learn Japanese to Be a Voice Actor," and that was a couple days' worth of projects that I thought I was just going to get done in 15 minutes, but over the time I was like this does not make any sense. And so, I just kept spending days working on it until it was about a week's worth of work, and it sounded and felt like what I wanted to say. That was the first article I've ever written somewhere outside of my own little circle. It had over 1000 people talking about it, in terms of comments and shares, so that was really interesting! (M. Richards, personal communication, August 20, 2020)

Sage's and Marley's experiences with learning are so very similar to how Kris and I have learned, and continue to learn, how to manage and lead ourselves and our time as entrepreneurs. The four of us spend a lot of time deschooling, noticing and naming schoolishness, and shifting in and out of both our collective and individual rhythms. I'll close with my understanding of some of the terms I've used here, in hopes that they will deepen your understanding of learning outside the confines of conventional ideas about learning.

Chapter 1

Unschooling: A child-trusting, anti-oppression, liberatory, love-centered approach to parenting and caregiving. It is also creating and expanding communities of confident, capable people who understand how they learn best, and how to work collaboratively to learn and solve things.

Deschooling: Shedding the programming and habits that resulted from other people's agency over your time, body, thoughts, or actions. Designing and practicing beliefs that align with your desire to thrive, be happy, and succeed.

Schoolishness: Conventional practices that are rooted in binaries, and generally accepted by adults, but rejected by children and teenagers, either overtly or covertly. A living out someone else's goals or narrative of how and what we should be. Schoolishness models an authoritarian approach to adult-child interaction as well as respectability ideas rooted in adults' innate superiority in knowledge.

Akilah S. Richards is passionate about mindful partnerships and decolonizing parenting. She started *Raising Free People Network*, a digital multimedia platform for education, deep listening, and emergent collaborations at the intersection of privilege, parenting, and power. Her unschooling podcast is called *Fare of the Free Child*, and her latest book, *Raising Free People:*

Akilah Richards

Unschooling as Liberation and Healing Work is
available through PM Press, many local bookstores, and
on Amazon.

Chapter 2

All Pulling in the Same Direction: How I Came to be a Gentle Parent and Home Educator

Rebecca English

Introduction

I'd like to begin this piece with three anecdotes that I think explain where I came from. My earliest memory is being about two or three. I must have done something naughty when I hear my father come home from work. I run out to tell him saying, "mummy is mad with me," as he bends down to greet me. I watch him stand upright and back away as my mother comes outside, grabs my wrist and yanks me so I'm looking her in the eyes as she says, "children never come between their parents." This message was reinforced on every trip to the shops, where we, my brother and I, were never allowed to walk between our parents, we were to walk a pace or two behind.

Anecdote 1

I remember being eight-years-old, on the vinyl seats in the back of our old Cortina, I am being driven to school. My mother and I are arguing, again, and I remember her saying that I should stop complaining, she remembers well how it feels to be an eight-year-old girl, after all, she'd been an eight-year-old girl too. I remember looking out the window at the flood-plain, now it's a golf-driving range but it used to just be grassland and a creek, thinking how there was no way

31

she could possibly remember what it's like to be eight, she's ancient. I also remember thinking I would never say that to a child of mine, in that moment I promised I would never tell any child of mine I knew how it felt to be a certain age. As it turns out, when I was eight she was 35, when she was eight the world was completely different. My grandmother had a saying, "I know you better than you know yourself," mum's thing about remembering what it was like to be eight was her way of saying she knew me better than I did and I should be quiet and do as I was told.

Anecdote 2

Now I'm in high school, an elite, all girls' catholic school in the middle of the city. It's a very nice school, and one that has an excellent reputation for turning out girls who become doctors, not girls who marry doctors. That doctor phrase is a thing where I live. I am in year eight, the first year of high school. I am walking up the hill through the school's back gate past the old "duck pond" which is what they used to call the school pool. The gate isn't there anymore and neither is the pool, it was filled in and replaced with a state-of-the-art water polo pool. I am deep in thought about my parents and I remember thinking, of my mother in particular that her advice and ideas were self-serving, and I should likely do the opposite of whatever she told me to do. My mother did all the parenting, my father was always studying or working or both. She was very strict and authoritarian and not very warm or loving or caring. She never held our hair if we were sick, they would lock their bedroom door at night so you'd have to bash on the wall to ask them to come help you if you needed them, and she would ignore you for weeks at a time if you slighted her. I remember knowing that, no matter what happened, if I had children, I would do the opposite of whatever they had done.

Anecdote 3

When I was 33-years-old, I fell pregnant with my first child. All those experiences suddenly became very real, and I had to now live up to being the mother I had always promised myself I would be.

Our Approach

Neil Postman, in his book, *The Disappearance of Childhood* (1996), states that childhood is "disappearing at a dazzling speed" (p. i). He then goes on to argue that, it is not so much childhood that is disappearing, but an affect of childhood; he is referring to the discourse of childhood that has existed, in Postman's words "for less than 400 years" (p. xi). For him childhood, which is often used to refer to "a special class of people somewhere between the ages of seven and, say, seventeen, requiring special forms of nurturing and protection, and believed to be qualitatively different from adults" has probably only existed, as we know it, for around "one hundred and fifty years" (Postman, 1996, p. xi).

Drawing on the work of Ariès (1996), the premise of Postman's argument is not that children themselves are new, but what is new is how we think of people we call children, how we expect them to behave, to act, to think, and to be. Ariès' (1996) work argues that childhood came into being around the seventeenth century in royal families and the very upper classes, over time, ideas about childhood trickled down so that, for the mass of the population, by the late nineteenth or early twentieth century people aged between seven and seventeen were considered to be, in Postman's words, qualitatively different from adults.

Taking that "age of reason" idea, and others who say that childhood is a social construction, we have always tried to make our children agents and give them responsibility for their own lives. We asked our children not whether they were excited about going to school but, rather, whether they wanted to go. When you give children agency over the decisions about how they are educated, you create a situation where you need to be prepared for them deciding they do not want to go to school.

I have three children. We home educate because my oldest child decided she did not want to go to school. Her brothers have both said they don't want to go either. People shudder when you tell them you asked your children if they wanted to go to school, probably because, as Epstein (2007) noted, most people's view of children are "propelled in part by the underlying belief— new in human history—that young people are helpless and incompetent" (p. 39). It is this idea that young people are helpless and incompetent and could not possibly know what they want, or how they think or what is best for them, that is new in human history, even the Catholic Church stated that by seven, a human had the ability to reason (Aries, 1996). We have been accused of taking a dreadful risk with our children's education from one set of parents and the other side has been accepting and, probably from watching hours of Fox News, doesn't believe schools are up to scratch in any event.

Researchers on unschooling highlight the differences in the verbs to and with, for example Ricci (2011) talks about the ways things are done to, not with, children. Adults design curriculum documents that determine when, how and what children ought to learn. Adults decide that all parents/guardians know best for their children, an example of that is the reliance on permission slips and "notes from home" that both permit and excuse children from activities. In order to be allowed to attend a school excursion, a child needs their parents'/guardians' permission form, dutifully filled out and signed. If a child is sick and needs a day off school, they need to be excused from a class or to explain why their homework is incomplete, a parent or guardian must authorize it and give their permission.

Where we live, we have very strict governmental control over home education. This law mirrors the ways that children are treated in schools and the curriculum they must study. Like schools, these rules take agency away from children and give it to an external body tasked with managing children's education. The law changed in 2016, without the government consulting the home education community, that made unschooling in Queensland very difficult to do legally (cf. English, 2020). The requirements for registration mean I have to ask my children to help me help them achieve their goal, staying home, by doing what the government asks. As a result, our home education includes some book work that mirrors school tasks. We do some work in the mornings, usually some maths and literacy (reading and writing) and some other subjects if we are interested in learning something particular. After that, we do some music practice, but this is usually left until the afternoon, and the rest of the day is free for play. On Mondays to Thursdays and Saturdays, the children do formal activities, taekwondo, music, dancing, activities they asked to do. The rest of their time is free.

We have to prepare a report every year for the government that shows my children have "learned something." Reports take a long time to prepare and are unnecessarily arduous. They need to be completed using a form the government education department provides, printed and posted to the section of the education department that is tasked with managing home education registrations prior to the completion of 10 months of home education. My reports run to 50 pages per child. It's a lot of work to complete them.

Our approach is determined by the government's requirements for registration, the children's desires for how they want to spend their days, their need to practice or go to their activities, and my husband and my need to work. Our approach is one that attempts to share agency between all members of the family so that children and adults are on an equal footing and all of us are affected by our obligations to each other. It is hard to fit work in, and to make time for the things I want to do, but the children have as much say over what happens in the house as the adults do, and if we believe we oughtn't elevate adults over children, this approach is the only way to reconcile our ideological position with the lived experiences of our family.

I agree with John Holt who stated we should allow our "children as much freedom to learn in the world as their parents can comfortably bear" (Holt, 2003). Following the work of Freire, we believe in a learner-centered pedagogical approach that sees our children as learning through dialogue and that, to impose learning on them without their consent, is an act of tyranny. I note the work of Freire (2000) who stated the problem with schools was that they attempt to bank knowledge in children so that the learner becomes a container, a *receptacle* which is *filled* by whatever has been determined that they must learn. Freire (2000) argued "the more completely [the teacher] fills the receptacles, the better a teacher she [sic] is" while, the corollary is "the more meekly the receptacles permit themselves to be filled, the better students they are" (p. 72).

Sadly, the requirements of the government reporting form that home educators in Queensland have to complete mirrors the banking concept of education. As Freire (2000) noted, this approach is oppressive and treats children as an object whose only role was to be "adaptable, manageable" while whoever was charged with teaching becomes all-powerful and has all the authority. We fight this approach by giving our children as much freedom as we can because we see "the more students work at storing the deposits entrusted to them, the less they develop the critical consciousness" to transform the world (Freire, 2000, p. 73). It concerns us that, as Freire (2000) argued, a banking approach to education required students to adapt to the world "as it is and to the fragmented view of reality deposited in them," rather than taking an active and agentive role in the world (p. 73). Agency is very important to me, I never experienced agency as a young person, and I was determined my children would have as much agency as I could give them as a parent. So, we manage their requirements in line with the government's mandates on how to report while giving them as much freedom as we can to do the things they love throughout the day.

I use sociological theory in my research and writing work. In my PhD, I used the work of Basil Bernstein. He argued that all communication is pedagogical because it is about trying to teach the receiver about the way the world works. In particular, he noted that communication acts as a carrier for more than facts, and contains information that is more than itself, "it is a carrier of power relations external to education," it is a "carrier for patterns of dominance" (Bernstein, 2000, p. 4). As such, all communication maintains symbolic control, a process whereby, "power relations are transformed into discourse and discourse into power relations" (Bernstein, 2000, p. xxvi). He argued that symbolic control was an attempt by those in power to "shape and distribute forms of consciousness, identity and desire" (Bernstein, 2000, p. 201). It is this idea of the shaping and forming of consciousness and identity that accords with Freire's work. Freire (2000) argued that humans are aware of themselves, as beings in the world and, through that awareness, they were conscious.

However, this consciousness exists in a dialectical relationship with the limits of their freedom. These relationships are in flux and struggle and, as such, link to notions of power. In much the same terms, Bernstein (2000) argued power relations "create boundaries, legitimize boundaries, reproduce categories of discourse, different categories of agents" (p. 5).

The Role of Education

It is my experience, having been a teacher and a teacher educator, a mother and a facilitator at home education co-ops, that the ways we educate children in mainstream schools in Australia acts to "shape consciousness differently" so that "power always operates to produce dislocations, to produce punctuations in social space" (Bernstein, 2000, p. 5). The role of education is to teach a child their place, so that they learn the limits of the thinkable, they learn to aspire to whatever the system makes reasonable for them. My cousin became a mechanic because, as he has often said, that was about as good a job as a boy like him, living in the housing commission outer western suburbs could aspire. Giving children agency also teaches a child their place, but it does so in a way that attunes their consciousness toward their own needs and beliefs, allows them the space to think about what they think of the world, and how they want the world to be, it gives them the freedom to be fully conscious (Freire, 2000). While classroom knowledge distributes power relations, specifically the power over "the unthinkable and the thinkable" while simultaneously "differentiate[ing] and stratify[ing] groups" (Bernstein, 2000, p. 31), our approach attempts to give our children the chance to think the unthinkable, to give them the power to, as Freire (2000) notes, "critically consider reality" (p. 74), and to consider ways to change the world or make a world for themselves that suits their individual needs.

We did not ever want our children to have their identities and their lives restricted by the mainstream school way of thinking and seeing the world. Our children are free to have their own world, where they imagine the ways things are and are free to create that world as they want, wherever their imagination takes them. They can play dragon riders, make imaginary watermelon smoothies, and build a fort under the front veranda. They can do all of this on their own terms, without the need to produce any artefact as evidence of a specific learning outcome linked to their activities, linked to curriculum. As Holt (2004, p. 120) stated:

> Why does there always have to be an outcome? When I go to see something that interests me, I don't have to do a dance afterwards or make a six-foot papier mâche map and hoist it up to the ceiling. I can decide what kind of outcome I want, if any, for my experience. More important, I can wait until the outcome reveals itself to me.

Our children's desire to stay at home and under no circumstances to be made to go to school allows them the time and the space to reveal what their experiences mean to them. It may not be my understanding of that experience, but my understanding is irrelevant. Children should have as much agency as an adult, they are just as fully human, even if they don't have as much experience or aren't quite as tall. As a parent, I see it as my job to give my children the space to unfurl their experiences in a way that reveals their understanding of the world. Anything else amounts to tyranny, it produces dislocations and punctuations, it classifies their experiences through the lens of my own, and it renders their ideas profane in relation to the sacred, where the sacred is whatever the adult thinks a child should be finding from their experience.

The Child

I recently was asked to do a *Radio National* interview about how parents manage the juggle of childcare when it's the long summer holidays. I went along, got all giddy when the interviewer was a famous radio and TV interviewer I'd seen many times, and participated in the discussion. The other interviewee was concerned that schools weren't keeping up with parents' time demands and weren't meeting parents' needs for childcare.

I asked, although both the interviewer and the other interviewee seemed nonplussed with this point, whether we didn't risk making school a euphemism for free child minding. After all, if our only concern was that parents' work hours were covered with school and ancillary services (such as outside school hours care), then what does that say about schools' role in our community, and, more broadly, where does education fit in this discussion?

I relate that anecdote because I think it raises the fundamental questions about living and experiencing with children. First, I think it suggests children are seen as somewhat of a burden, one that gets in the way of parents' other commitments, specifically work. If the community are more concerned about how children are a burden on their parents' time, then how highly do we value good parenting? And, what does that communicate to children about their worth? Second, it appears that parents' roles as workers, as units of labour in service of an employer, is more highly valued than their role as parents. Third, I wonder about what education means in this kind of environment. Interestingly, when you tell people you home educate, their response is often along the lines of, "I can only imagine it's better for your kids' education." The interview experience suggested to me that Australians acknowledge that schools are failing educationally in many cases and that they are glorified childcare centres in some cases too, whose role is to give parents a break so they can work on their more important job, their paid job.

A lot of people also say they couldn't home educate. They don't have time, have the money or the resources or they don't know how to teach. For many, they say they couldn't do it because they would go mad or they'd hate their kids even more. I have given up responding to those questions, but do feel pretty badly when they say they'd go crazy or hate their kids in front of . . . the kids. I try to communicate both pity and support to the kids, but I don't know if my weak smile cuts the mustard.

Chapter 2

I am lucky, I have three awesome young people who live with my husband and me. They are fantastic company, we all help each other out, and do our best to make each other's journey easy. The advantages about our not sending children to school include not having to force them to get up and get a uniform on to go to school. Uniforms are mandatory here in Australia in most cases, and my children have said how ugly and restrictive they are. My daughter would likely have to wear a dress, if not by school policy but by peer pressure, and my sons would have to cut their hair. We don't have to force them to do homework. I don't have to watch them have their personalities affected by gruelling schooling schedules, an overreliance on standardised teaching approaches or the nationalised testing regime. They can go to taekwondo of an afternoon without the day hanging over them so they can learn that skill. They have time to practice piano and violin. They can imagine their world. They don't worry that they are dumb because they haven't grasped some concept in the time the system determined was the right time. My daughter proudly states she has dyslexia and that's why she doesn't read well yet.

When I work, I am lucky enough to be able to afford to have a babysitter sit with my children. It isn't cheap and I am lucky enough that I have a flexible job. I am lucky that my husband also has a flexible job and he's on board with approaching children from a place of respect and agency. I don't worry if they're sick, what on earth I am going to do about work today. I don't worry about taking the children on holidays because I don't report to anyone, I don't need to seek permission from a principal, or a school board to go during term time.

Our arrangement is working for us, but I know it wouldn't work for everyone. Our main concerns, as parents, is agency and respect. We respect our children's needs and try, wherever possible, to honour their agency over their lives. The decision wasn't really ours to make, and we discuss negotiation and respect with the children. It's respect that means they need to tidy up the house, it's a shared space. Home education is a furtherance of our only rule, respect, because it is about respecting the children and their needs and wants, we are all respectful of each other because we are working together to ensure our family is a group that pulls in the same direction.

Dr. Rebecca English is a researcher, teacher, and mother whose work is concerned with parenting and education. She has an interest in the ways parents make choices for their children that align with their beliefs about family, parenting and other factors. Rebecca has been teaching for 20 years. She has worked with a number of different schools teaching in the senior-secondary and middle years. In 2021, she edited a book on home education, *Global Perspectives on Home Education in the 21st Century*. In 2022, she published a co-authored book, *The Superwoman Myth: Can Contemporary Women Have It All Now?* She continues to publish widely in academic and popular press. She has been interviewed for television programs such as *The Project*, *ABC Mornings* and *SBS/Vice's* short productions as well as dailies including the *Sydney Morning Herald, Courier Mail* and various other publications. She is currently writing a book on gentle parenting.

Robin Alpern

The School of Benign Neglect

Robin Alpern

In service to capitalism and the desire for automatons to work the factories and mills, our country developed a model of education in the 1800s that forced children in lock-step through a series of cookie cutter molds. The system was designed to produce workers who would do as they were told, when and how and where they were told. Not nearly enough has changed since then.

When the time came in the 1980s for my then-husband Bowen and me to educate our own children, we made a break for freedom and chose unschooling. Dispensing with curricula, lessons, schedules, textbooks, tests, grades, and professional teachers, we raised our four kids in a program I secretly named the School of Benign Neglect. A place for them to live and learn, guided by their interests, abilities, instincts, and internal timetables. We would offer them support, resources, and occasional direction.

It was a dangerous plan, allowing our children to steer their own way, risking their future happiness and success. We took the chance, because it seemed to suit our children and our family style, and because we believed many of the worst ills of our society arise from institutions, such as schools, that prioritize products and profits over human beings.

In the process, I co-founded Tri-County Homeschoolers, a network that eventually comprised hundreds of families spread across three states. It was the village we needed for raising and educating our children.

~ ~ ~

Our homeschool adventure had its roots in my childhood. I was the middle of three daughters in a family that was mainstream in many respects: a white, American, middle-class, Protestant nuclear family with two able-bodied, heterosexual, cis-gender, college-educated parents. However, our family was consciously and committedly nonconformist: Quaker, pacifist, vegetarian, racially aware, politically active. That set us apart from the conservative, predominantly white upstate New York town I grew up in. One more factor was that I was born in 1954 and came of age in the sixties, when "Question Authority" wasn't just a bumper sticker, but a national pastime.

So maybe it wasn't surprising that by the time I reached my late teens, I was critiquing our educational system. In a flash of insight while reading *Siddhartha* by Hermann Hesse, I realized that although I was a high school senior with straight A's, I had never been taught in school to think. I studied John Holt's books on school reform, interviewed proponents of an "open school" for our town (it never happened), and won first prize from the school magazine for an essay titled "Caution: School May Be Hazardous to Your Health." While my sisters and I received a conventional education, my mother said later that if homeschooling had been an option, she would have seized it.

Years later, in 1987, Bowen and I were expecting our first child. My sister gifted me a book about midwife-assisted homebirth and I was hooked. Lincoln was born at home that October. This is significant to our homeschool story. Bucking the medical system to control my birthing experience empowered me to believe I could direct my child's upbringing. Why give away the joy of educating him to strangers?

A small miracle led me to a neighbor, Liz Whitten-Snarr, who planned to homeschool her two-year-old son Bertie. Liz informed me Holt had given up on improving schools and turned to homeschooling. I knew immediately this was the path I wanted for our family.

Over the next couple of years, Liz and I explored possibilities. Our La Leche League leader, Georgianna Stucchio, had read *Summerhill*, the classic book by Alexander Neill about his experimental school in England. As a result she enrolled her children, Christian and Susannah, in a Montessori School. But she was dissatisfied with their experience there. She suggested we talk with Linda Carroll, a professional with a strong interest in alternative education. Our commitment to home education began to gel. Not just a crazy notion for people far away in England, it was something we could and wanted to do.

The Growth of a Movement

Our budding network coalesced formally around the spring of 1990. Beryl Polin, another LLL member, hosted a meeting numbering eleven families. Rejecting the notion of "schooling" our children in any form, we named ourselves the Westchester Home Learners (WHL). We agreed to meet twice a month, at different times of day to accommodate varying schedules, and also fathers with day jobs.

Years later, in 2007, founders of the group gathered to reconstruct our history. One person described those early years of our network as "halcyon days." For families with enough resources, good health and some luck, the years of raising children are bound to have a special glow. In the case of our members, I believe the glow was augmented by our carving out a brave new world. Homeschooling was a challenge not only to society, but to our own sense of ourselves. We had grown up with traditional schooling, and the style of parenting that accompanied it. Every step we took as homeschoolers was on uncharted territory—or felt that way. The risks and rewards were high, adding that golden luster to people, places, and activities that made up our pioneer adventure.

In the spring of 1992, Liz hosted a meeting with Jerry Mintz, founder of the Alternative Education Resource Organization. We discussed forming a learning cooperative. The meeting led to two significant developments. One was that Betsy Lewis, from a homeschool group across the river in Rockland County, volunteered to create a calendar of events. Over the next several years, Betsy's print calendar arriving in the mail each month kept us connected and flourishing. Second, after the meeting with Jerry, a little WHL band crossed the Hudson to attend a meeting of the Rockland group. Thus, we formed the kernel of Tri-County Homeschoolers (TCH), with members in Westchester, Rockland, and Orange Counties. We remained TCH for many years, morphing into the Tri-State Homeschoolers when we acknowledged our membership spread across New York State, Connecticut, and New Jersey.

There was mild tension between our groups in the beginning. Homeschoolers from Rockland and Orange focused more on traditional schooling and organization, while in Westchester many of us embraced unschooling. However, we began to cross-pollinate successfully, with more players and more places to go.

In the fall of 1992, our family moved to Ithaca, NY, where Bowen was on sabbatical for a year. We were now a family of four, our daughter Julian having been born at home a year earlier. With an infant to care for, a brand-new community without my network of support, and an international elementary school one block away, I caved and enrolled Lincoln in kindergarten. He loved it! Until he didn't. After Christmas vacation, he began objecting to school. To their credit, school officials tried to make changes to accommodate Lincoln's wishes, such as allowing him to read a book during mandatory nap time. Despite this, Lincoln continued to protest. Bowen and I took a deep breath, and withdrew him from school.

The Courage To Do What is Needed

I was terrified and elated. I drew confidence from realizing I was a happy, functioning adult who didn't know everything . . . but enough to make my way through life. It seemed possible Bowen and I could support our children to learn what they needed to be happy and accomplished too.

Chapter 3

From the beginning, I had no interest in teaching
Lincoln following a curriculum. I wanted our family to
simply enjoy life together, without defining formal
educational projects or specific class schedules. But
would that be enough? An immediate concern, since I
came from a highly literary family, was that Lincoln had
left kindergarten before they taught the alphabet.
Without structured lessons, how would he learn it?
Before long though, I discovered he'd learned on his
own, through simple observation. It made sense that
children, built for survival, would absorb from their
environment much of what they needed to know.

When we returned to Peekskill in the fall of
1993, we reconnected with TCH. One member, Lane
Lynn, was a proponent of unschooling. She fortified my
conviction that "live and learn" was not a platitude, but a
reality and a strategy for education. I knew
homeschoolers who scheduled regular times for daily
classes on well-defined subjects, based on approved
curricula. That was not for us! I thought school was a
poor model for education and certainly didn't want to
recreate it at home. I would not have felt comfortable
trying to "teach" my son in such artificial circumstances,
and it was clear he wouldn't have accepted that kind of
relationship or structure. Instead we played together, did
housework, went on errands, joined TCH outings, visited
family and friends. When strangers would ask wide-eyed
about homeschooling, I would inform them, "Right now,
this grocery store (library/playground/etc.) is our
classroom. And you're the teacher!"

Lincoln was about to turn six, the legal age of
compulsory education. It was time to officially stake our

Robin Alpern

claim as home educators. In NYS that required sending the school superintendent a "letter of intent" to homeschool. We wrote that we didn't separate Lincoln as a learner from the rest of our family, and that we all expected to gain an education.

Tri-County Homeschoolers

I felt truly fortunate TCH had blossomed into a network of dozens of families with a rich variety of events and activities. Many were attended by parents with children of all ages, so I could bring both my six-year-old and my toddler, and we would all have a good time. Over the years our monthly bulletin filled with opportunities including sports, nature programs, math and chess clubs, art and craft classes, science classes, reading and writing clubs, law classes, theater programs and more. Most were organized by parents, but sometimes kids led activities or taught classes.

Two events that grew over the years into major hubs for our group were the weekly ice skating in winter at the Bear Mountain rink, and Wednesdays at the Garrison Art Center (GAC). GAC sits on the banks of the Hudson River, surrounded by beautiful lawns, where moms and dads would hang out and picnic with the younger kids while their older siblings were in pottery, sewing, or drawing classes. We spent so many communal hours playing, brainstorming problems, sharing resources, venting, and making friends. At the rink adults had a chance to catch up with each other while kids played tag and crack the whip.

Chapter 3

Because we were a community, people helped
each other out in all sorts of ways. This became
especially evident to me in the summer of 1997, when
my third child turned out to be fraternal twins, Guinevere
and Emrigael. Homeschoolers organized meal deliveries,
and Mary Ann Baiyor (who later became publisher of
the monthly bulletin) visited weekly with her two
daughters to help with housework. When I finally dared
bring the twins as three-year-olds to Bear Mountain,
Frank Adams—himself the father of much older twin
boys—provided the extra hands I needed to manage so
many kids on the ice.

Learning to Read

I've often been asked how our children learned to
read. Of course, the journey was different for each of
them, and I honestly don't remember a lot of detail,
partly because it went well. I was fortunate to be
introduced early on to Frank Smith's book, *Reading
Without Nonsense*. Smith confirmed children can learn to
read without formal instruction, and at whatever age they
are ready, as opposed to the age dictated by school
curricula.

Bowen and I enjoyed reading aloud. He read
Lincoln *The Hobbit* when he was four. Not all children
would be interested, but Lincoln ate it up. He also
discovered books on tape and listened to them by the
hour. By the time he was six, despite Frank Smith's
assurances there was no hurry, we felt somewhat
pressured to teach Lincoln to read. He didn't seem
motivated. Bowen had the idea to read *Call of the Wild*

aloud, and once Lincoln was hooked on the story, we got him a large print copy he could read along with. From there he progressed rapidly. That same year, Bowen read Lincoln the entire trilogy of the *Lord of the Rings*. Our son began borrowing the book on tape from the library, playing it repeatedly. He also started writing stories of his own. It was evident he was picking up literary devices and rhythms from listening to so much literature. Lincoln has become a masterful writer, owing to thousands of hours spent reading as a child.

Back to School, For a While

Julian, meanwhile, got the urge at age six to go to school. For a year she badgered me. Though I felt it was an unhealthy choice, I agreed finally, since my prime principle was to follow her lead. She was happy at first in second grade. But before long she had complaints: the teacher scolded students harshly; there was too much homework and pressure to complete it on time; some kids were mean. I hated nagging her to do homework, and supporting other unpleasant aspects of school, when I disapproved of the whole system. The day she came home upset once again in her sixth week, I suggested it was time to withdraw. Unfortunately, the lice she picked up at school and shared with our whole family lasted nine weeks. It did not endear me to school.

However, one gift from her teacher was a reading trick, a method of "stretching out the words." That worked, and Julian took to devouring books.

Teaching the twins to read was both easier and harder. Harder because the girls did not sit for hours listening to books. I didn't know what to do with them! I let them play as they wanted and trusted they'd learn what they needed. This was easier because I'd already seen my older children learn by osmosis. Eventually the twins were reading plenty. Guinevere was slower to pick it up, until Julian introduced her to a favorite fantasy series. Soon Guinevere was plowing through the books.

It was during Julian's stint in second grade that I realized school might work perfectly well for many families; it just was not my family's style. Schools and teachers have afforded a great deal to a great many students. In our case, homeschooling allowed me to parent in a way that worked for me, and appeared to nourish my children. I began thinking of my model as the school of benign neglect. I worked hard at raising my children; it's just that my method relied less on directing, controlling or pushing, and more on staying out of my children's way. Over the years, each of my children has been repeatedly complimented on their intelligence. While I'm very proud of them, I believe all children are naturally brilliant. Unfortunately, much of what happens to them in school can dull or severely damage that innate intelligence.

Common Thoughts

Bowen and I never worried about trying to make our children study all of the traditional subject areas. I knew I'd spent untold hours in school studying material I never used again, at the cost of doing things that deepened and fulfilled me. In reality, nobody needs to know everything! Contrary to indoctrination by our educational system, we actually don't even really need to be well-rounded to live a satisfying life and contribute to society. Demanding that kids learn things they aren't interested in does not guarantee they will learn. It may well turn them against the subject. And life has a way of insisting if there's something we need to know outside our normal interests. So we largely trusted our children to chart their course themselves. Over the years they found a variety of modes for learning. When you are not confined to an institution for a significant portion of every day, the possibilities are limitless. And because you've chosen for yourself, you're more likely to learn. For instance, in their teens, the twins discovered free online classes at programs such as Kahn Academy, Crash Course, and DuoLingo. They spent hours studying a range of subjects at their own pace and entirely voluntarily.

Probably the biggest question I've heard over the years was what about social life? This is predicated on the belief schools socialize children and do a good job. Think hard about your own experience. Children in school face some or all of the following: peer pressure, typecasting (bully, sissy, teacher's pet, nerd, class clown, dummy, jock, etc.), isolation from family and friends, segregation from children of other ages, minimized attention from adults, an atmosphere of competition rather than cooperation, and violence ranging from spitballs and name-calling to guns. Is this really an ideal environment for socialization?

Humans are social animals. Socializing is in our hard wiring. We need a lot of fine tuning, but it's not like our children are starting from scratch. Parents who are home educating (that is, raising) their children have the opportunity to observe closely what skills their children possess and what needs improvement. And without a constant throng of other children to tend, home educators can teach or model social skills through everyday family activities, in and out of the house. My son in his tween years puttered alone in his room all day, building Legos, writing comic books and reading. His younger sister desired constant companionship and attracted the entire neighborhood to our house. My socializing strategies for them were obviously quite different. I scheduled classes and forays out in the world for my son, and periods of solitude for my daughter. With my son, I focused on developing respect and communication skills to help him navigate the gap between him and others. With my daughter, I worked more on handling feelings that arise through the ups and downs of friendships.

Of course, our homeschool village socialized the kids in profound ways. When Lincoln turned eight, he wrote a guest list for the birthday party comprised of several entire families. He was friends not only with children his age, but also with their older and younger siblings, their parents and in some cases extended family. How beautiful not to be limited to people born the same year, and to know people in the context of their families.

Once when Lincoln played with a friend who attended school, I noticed how competitive the friend was. While that was only one instance, it contrasted with TCH norms of cooperation and collaboration. Those were values I wanted my children to hold, and it was much easier when we were surrounded by people who shared them.

Another generally held value in TCH was for parents to follow and support their children's lead. As a person who detests telling others what to do, this way of educating suited me. But it was possible because I had partners in TCH with whom I could discuss problems, questions, theories, resources. Unschooling was especially scary, because it was such a departure from the educational model within which everyone I knew grew up. I often returned to Lane Lynn with questions, and her steadfast confidence in our children's innate capacities for learning and directing their own education convinced me to stick to it. Also, for many years Lisa Heyman led an unschooling support group that was vital for addressing issues and finding companionship. As my kids grew older, Grace Llewellyn's book *The Teenage Liberation Handbook* demonstrated the brilliance of teens in designing their own educational journey, with assistance from family and community.

Unschooling Outcomes

My children now range in age from 23 to 33. All attended or are currently in college. The transition from unschooling to full-time college classes was different for each child, of course.

Lincoln was limited in schools he could apply to because of his lack of high school transcript. He was accepted at Antioch College in Ohio, perhaps the best possible match for him. His application was helped by the fact the admissions officer was a homeschool parent. Tragically, Antioch closed after Lincoln's freshman year. He found other ways to continue his formal education, but never graduated. Some years later, he was accepted into a degree program in Postcolonial Culture and Global Policy in London and emerged with his Master's—without ever having earned a Bachelor's degree. What a perfect unschooling outcome.

Julian, meanwhile, experimented with school again in the ninth grade. As in second grade, she found much she liked, and a lot she hated. One day she told me, "School is deadening my soul." After that I found it truly hard to drag her out of bed each morning and force her out the door. She quit high school after two weeks. Soon she created her own academic regimen, hauling books and papers to the living room every morning and poring over subjects ranging from history to German language. At age 16 she found a passion for the Russian language. She obtained special permission to take a class at nearby Vassar College with a native Russian speaker. That experience inspired her to apply to college. She was more frustrated than Lincoln by her lack of a high school diploma or transcript since she wasn't eligible to apply for any of the colleges that appealed to her. In the end she chose one that offered great study abroad opportunities. She had developed discipline and focus, but lacked skills learned in school such as note-taking, writing papers, making presentations, and test-taking. She acquired these overnight though, and graduated with honors four years later.

My only child to attend (and remain in) school before college was Emrigael, who entered the ninth grade and stayed through graduation. A consistent honor roll student with a diploma, she obviously had the easiest time getting into and succeeding in college. She will enter her senior year this fall, and has made the Dean's list almost every semester.

Guinevere resolutely avoided school, but received tutoring in her high school years when we realized she was mildly dyslexic. Eventually I persuaded her to take a single class in her favorite subject, graphic art, at our community college. She enrolled non-matric to keep the stakes low. Loving the work, she excelled in class and returned for an advanced drawing class the next semester. She then felt ready to enroll full-time, and is now acing her way through a liberal arts education.

The Challenges

Though I wouldn't trade our school of benign neglect for any other, our family has experienced some significant downsides to home education. Guinevere's dyslexia would have been diagnosed much earlier in school and would not have held her back so long. Lincoln realized as an adult that he was *not* happily puttering in his room all those teen years; he felt lonely and isolated. Because he has learning differences, it's not clear he would have thrived in school either. But perhaps he would have had a better shot at finding friends and activities. Julian felt keenly the lack of structured education in the company of others and regretted I had not been more supportive of her attempts to succeed in school. Bowen and I didn't work hard to expose our children to subject areas outside our interests—it wasn't till she had to fulfill college pre-requisites that Guinevere discovered her love of earth science and biology. As adults, both Lincoln and Julian have been denied access to employment and higher education opportunities because of their lack of a high school diploma and/or Bachelor's degree, despite other documentation of their scholastic excellence. This points to serious flaws, not in home education, but in our society's institutions. Still, our family did finally learn the lesson. During Guinevere's teens, she took the Test Assessing Secondary Completion to obtain her high school equivalency.

The Benefits

Despite those drawbacks, we also reaped so many rewards from homeschooling. Our children all developed a strong sense of self through having the freedom to determine so much of how to spend their time and energy. This gift is especially important for girls who, in our patriarchal culture, tend to lose their voice and agency by the time they reach their teens. My daughters are each strong, self-assured individuals. (Susannah Sheffer, author of *A Sense of Self: Listening to Homeschooled Adolescent Girls,* documents that self-esteem seems particularly high among homeschooled girls.)

Some of my children have neurological anomalies and/or learning differences. I believe in school they might have been subjected to teasing and shaming at best, and bullying at worst. Homeschooling allowed my children to grow up with respect and appreciation for who they were and how they behaved, even if that didn't conform to norms. Some will argue we need the school of hard knocks to learn to be strong. What if growing up in your family and community with love makes you grounded, resourceful, resilient, and healthy?

Freedom from school schedules allowed our family to travel, spend time together and with friends, get involved in our community, and take up hobbies like acting, writing, pottery and Japanese kanji. As an eight-year-old, Julian became best friends with another homeschooler, Siobhan McGee. The two of them were joined at the hip for the next five years and would take turns staying for days in each other's homes, because they weren't required to report to school. Most children never have the opportunity to develop such friendships because they simply do not have the luxury of time.

In writing this chapter, I asked my children to name something they gained from homeschooling. Guinevere appreciates that she was allowed to discover the pleasure of learning as a way to enrich her life, rather than as a means to meet abstract or externally prescribed goals. She added that she feels she is more self-aware than many of her peers, as a result of growing up discerning her own needs, abilities and preferences, and choosing her activities.

Emrigael experimented with middle school when she was thirteen. She withdrew after four days, but that was enough to get a taste of mean girl culture. She is grateful now she didn't spend her teens surrounded by peers who think it's cool being spiteful to others.

Julian recalls many of her friends disliked reading since they were forced to learn in school, and assigned what to read. Books are one of her chief pleasures to this day.

Lincoln feels he would not have been as likely to enjoy topics such as history and social studies the way they are taught in school. Freedom to explore on his own terms made these subjects potent areas of interest.

One of my goals in homeschooling was to teach my children a major life skill: knowing how to find information. Then we entered the Information Age, where no one needs to know their way around a phone book, encyclopedia, thesaurus, or any other resource. Simply google it! However, growing up with the chance to think for themselves, all four children developed extraordinary gifts of critique. They are among my finest teachers, expertly cracking the codes and subtext behind media, current events and politics, and making informed decisions.

Raising and educating children is a long game. The results may take generations to come in. After roughly thirty years of Benign Neglect, I'm inclined to call our experiment a triumph.

Robin Mallison Alpern is a 68-year-old woman who narrowly missed a career as an elementary school teacher. Instead, she and her former husband unschooled their four children to college. Robin co-founded Tri-State Homeschoolers, a large homeschooling organization in New York State. She has worked for the past twelve years at the multiracial anti-racist organization, Center for the Study of White American Culture, where she serves as Director of Training.

Navigating Self-Directed Education: One Family's Journey Through Learning and Life

Kate Green

It is no surprise that our current identified approach to learning fits within the Worldschooling ideology, as for our family, learning has been, and still is, a journey. We have traveled, not only across continents, but through educational approaches and styles incorporating the multiple interests of a large and eclectic family.

My five children were born in varying locations around the world and their learning has been an individual journey of discovery and exploration. Ranging in age from 34 down to 16, they have navigated multiple learning experiences which were primarily nested within an unschooling framework such as that initially espoused by the likes of John Holt and Ivan Illich. Our approach is eclectic but as a researcher and academic myself I am aware of how much influence came from the experiential learning embedded in the theories of such people as John Dewey, Carl Rogers, and Paulo Freire.

I learned about these theorists early on as I hail from a family of educators beginning with my grandmother who led the way as a teacher and headmistress in England for more than 50 years! My mother is a teacher and former director of special education, and I have a sister and brother who are in the education field. I teach in higher education degree programs and have done for almost 25 years now. I love researching and teaching about the learning process and enjoy working with educators to introduce and expand their thinking about self-directed and experiential learning. Often schools of education do not include these wider texts or videos and so I enjoy exposing novice educators to classics such as Holt or Freire and Summerhill/Democratic Schools . . . and new work such as that of Sugata Mitra and Salman Khan who are taking technology and exploring how we can use it to our advantage by personalizing learning that allows for greater self-direction.

While I have this love of learning in more alternative approaches, I embraced and excelled within the traditional education systems. I went from an associates' degree in journalism while in the US Air Force (USAF) to a bachelors in psychology, master's in education and then combined the two interests into a PhD in child development. I love learning and I am lucky that my cognitive style aligns with traditional systems. We know so much now about how these systems fail many people and yet we constantly perpetuate the cycle in academia. Hopefully now that more and more families are discovering the magic of self-directed/determined learning, we will see the stories and celebrate the accomplishments of these "graduates" such as those we are discovering in this book.

So how did our family move from the socially acceptable norms of "baby-daycare-preschool-public-school . . ." world? I think it all started when I held my first baby in the hospital and cried because I knew that I couldn't stand to leave him in someone else's care. The intensity of the attachment was beyond anything I had

Kate Green

anticipated as I'd been raised on Women's Liberation/Smashing the Glass Ceiling/Working Mother magazine and more. I had two strong women who raised me and were highly respected career women. I had just won multiple awards for journalism (named Best News writer in the Air Force) and taken the paper I was editor for to being named top in the Air Force. I was on a roll and offered jobs at the Pentagon and *Stars and Stripes Europe Newspaper*. But holding that 7.5 pounds of rather cone-headed (long labor!), splotchy newborn, I knew with an intensity that the main role I wanted then in my life was to mother and raise this child.

Of course, the USAF did not quite agree with me and so I found an excellent home daycare provider who I'm still in contact with today. She helped get me through the hours of leaving him and celebrated his accomplishments with our family. However, when she left the base and I was pregnant with our second child, I decided to leave the Air Force and focus on parenting and my own education. This was all in progression as my first two sons were growing and happily learning via play: books, dress up, blocks, clay, paint . . . all clearly providing a rich environment in which to learn about the world and even academics.

The Start of School?

I was really pushed by society and family to start the oldest in preschool. He was eager to learn but clearly not ready for the separations and cried passionately. I was told by extended family, teachers, and parenting books that we needed to push through and just leave him. I did and he eventually stopped crying but I still feel his pain to this day that I was not empowered enough to listen to his "voice" and not push him into the preschool.

His first year in kindergarten was also quite an experience. He entered school reading and doing math at about the 3rd grade level (all of his own doing rather than pushy parents) but sadly his public-school teacher could not accommodate his learning and he progressed from being bored and too talkative, to shutting down and just sitting. We were told by the gifted and talented director that because there were no programs for him until 3rd grade, we should seek out private schooling or look into homeschooling. The gifted private school looked wonderful but even with the 50% scholarship was out of our scope since I was in the midst of getting my master's degree. I remember speaking with the leader of a local homeschooling group one entire evening (I wish I knew her name to thank her now) about what this entailed and how it was possible as I'd never heard of this as an option. Remember this was pre-Internet (gasp). I put the phone down and went into my five-year-old son's bedroom and asked "how would you like to quit school and learn at home?" His entire body changed as he leaped out of bed and molded himself to me while sobbing "yes." I listened to that and he didn't go back. My second son loved his preschool at the time and he chose to continue for a couple more months until he too decided that lazy mornings reading in bed, climbing the mango tree in the backyard, scooping up sea life at the ocean, and spending his days in playful learning were more fun. And thus, our life of traversing alternative paths to learning began but more importantly I learned to follow my children's lead and listen to what we all needed.

I think that learning to listen and trust in your children's ability to learn from a self-directed perspective has been the biggest process for me and occasionally for them. We started out using a thematic unit approach, which at the beginning was fun for me to create and push them through. I still know far more about coral reefs and the Oregon Trail than I would have, had I not spent hours creating and teaching these units. But I can't really say that my children have a similar depth of knowledge from it just as I cannot recite all the English monarchs and dates of their rules that I had to memorize in elementary school. The units were fun for schoolish-me and okay for my kids but we soon fell into power struggles and mom-as-teacher role which just did not align with our attachment parenting beliefs and practices. It felt as if I wore multiple hats and each one had a different personality. My children often weren't sure which one I was wearing and it was during these times of disconnection that we experienced more emotional conflict. I realized that during the "off" times of our learning, such as when I was focusing on my own school work, the boys were actually engaging far more deeply with playful learning and we relaxed and enjoyed being together more. When I let go of controlling their learning, they were able to take ownership of it and so of course were more active and excited about the process.

Grown Unschoolers

Chapter 4

And so, we are now in about our 28th year of unschooling and I wouldn't have changed anything really except to have let go immediately (we did after about the first year) and relax while trusting in the process. We are unschoolers but discovered the term worldschooling which probably fits better as we've traveled the world for their father's job, my work, and now, because I work fully online, we travel because we are interested in places. We are all dual passport holders (UK and US) and also identify as Third Culture Kids because we've all lived out of our primary passport country multiple times. Two of my five are still living at home but the older three are out successfully navigating the world. All five have similar education journeys and yet had the freedom to learn at their own pace and find their place in the world.

Sam, my oldest (born in Texas), and the catalyst to our family discovering the homeschooling journey, was accepted into and got a full scholarship to the University of Tennessee, Knoxville (UTK) in physics and jazz guitar. He's a very talented musician in addition to loving math and science. He was the adolescent who read everything from Nietzsche to Shakespeare to Chaos Theory for fun. He decided at the end of his second year at UTK that it just wasn't an optimum fit for him and so swapped to the culinary institute of the university and got his diploma there. He's been a chef since then across a few US states and in various cuisines although now he is transitioning into the tech field.

My second oldest, Jake (born in the UK), spent about a year at community college and then we all went to Costa Rica for a few months and while there he decided that he wanted to travel and do some volunteer work. He saved up money and then found an opportunity in Peru at an orphanage and later with an Indian restaurant owner who delivered free meals to poverty stricken rural villages a few times a week. Both experiences garnered him strong mentors and international experiences plus the opportunity of working with food in a cross-cultural environment. When he arrived back to the US he applied and was accepted into a few liberal-arts universities before deciding on Oglethorpe University in Atlanta. He studied sociology there, minored in Spanish and did a semester in Germany which he loved. After leaving Oglethorpe he moved to Dubai with me and his siblings where he decided to follow in his uncle's career path (uncle was living in Dubai already) and also be a chef! Jake has worked in Dubai, Atlanta, two years in Oaxaca, Mexico, and now is in Melbourne, Australia working as an executive chef running a couple of top restaurants. So, with no formal training he has worked his way up to a top job in about five years.

My third son, Ben (born in Hawaii), never attended any formal school until age 17 when he jumped in and earned his associates degree in Dubai (I was helping to open a new university there so he was able to attend). He then finished his BS in International Studies at the University of South Florida and then a computer science masters' degree at DePaul University. He is now loving his work in UX and being a digital nomad. Ben is a gamer and spent much of his adolescence attached to a video game screen. He is living proof that gamers do go onto experience the world outside of that screen! He has friends all over the world and is a comfortable expat/traveler and third culture kid/young adult.

My fourth son, Max (born in the United Arab Emirates) is 19 and has always learned independently through an unschooling lens. He and his sister spent a year in a small alternative Waldorf school in Dubai (run by homeschoolers) and did take online synchronous math classes with a wonderful teacher. He has also chosen to take various other online courses and is particularly interested in philosophy, politics, psychology, and all things gaming and Manga. He's also studied Japanese, Korean, and Spanish online and face-to-face. He is now working on a bachelors in cyber security studying online from our new home in Mexico.

My fifth child and only girl, Charlotte (born in Tennessee), is 16 and the only truly sporty person in the family! She has gone from dance to ice skating to tennis and now all things horses and soccer. She is a very talented equestrian and has ridden and taken lessons in the UAE, England, Spain, Mexico, Thailand, South Africa, Slovenia, and the US. Equestrians seem to connect in a whole separate language and she is never daunted riding a new horse or taking a lesson in a foreign language with an unknown instructor. She also just spent a year playing for the American University of Sharjah soccer team while we were living on campus this last year for my job as a visiting professor. She is continuing both riding and soccer now in Mexico (and who knows what else). Worldschooling allows her to follow her interests and be immersed in the topics she loves.

Kate Green

It's fascinating for me to reflect back on the similarities and differences of all five of my children's learning journey. We've shared many of the same read-aloud book series together, watched videos that some enjoyed and some didn't, pulled out the same games or science kits, and even some of the same arts and crafts materials over the years. I love hearing a question from one of the younger ones and being able to say "well your brother found this book helpful" and share it. There is a continuity and flow of learning that because it's been so much a part of our daily lives, has helped to solidify our family into a more cohesive and connected unit.

We know that our environment shapes who we are and the people we engage with directly influence our development across all domains. I can see that even though all five of mine were able to choose their own learning, they were influenced by the materials, friends, and our family outlook toward learning. This is only natural and so as parents who do opt for self-directed paths, we need to be cognizant of the need to strew the environment with a variety of ideas and materials. Worldschooling has allowed us to do this so well because in travel and living in other countries we have all had experiences that I could not have envisioned.

We have been/are able to really engage in experiential learning via cultural immersion which circles back to my beliefs about unschooling and that children need to follow their own interests in developmentally appropriate ways. I'm a fan of David Kolb's Experiential Learning Theory (built on the backs of scholars such as John Dewey, Carl Jung, Lev Vygotsky, Carl Rogers, and Paulo Freire) which defines learning as "the process whereby knowledge is created through the transformation of experience. Knowledge results from the combination of grasping and transforming experience" (Kolb, 1984. p. 41). The theory goes on to explain that it takes time and freedom for experiences to cognitively translate into learning and that allowing learners to be in charge of their progress means they can allocate the practice time to develop expertise if so desired. I remember years ago reading John Holt's own journey to study the cello as an adult and wondering if my children would ever find hobbies they were passionate about and dig into this self-direction. At the time, they seemed only to be focused on mud pies, Disney movies, and Lego building. But now in comparing that to watching three of my son's love of music, my daughter's riding, and one son's quest to make the best mead and wine (among many other interests), I can clearly see how valuable it has been to give them this open learning space.

The Learning Journey

I'm writing this and reflecting back on our learning journey for the last three decades while in lock-down for COVID-19. We have been in our Florida home for two weeks now with only a couple of forays to do a grocery store curbside pick-up and there is no projected end date. Given that we unschool and any classes that my two teens take (math and veterinary science at the moment) are online and I work fully online teaching doctoral and master's level classes, our lives are not terribly uprooted. We lean toward being introverts and enjoy being together thus when not traveling we tend to putter around the house working on various projects of our own. There is a flow to our days that is normally quiet and relaxed with pleasant conversation and laughter. We like to cook and try new foods and recipes, many of which we have picked up as we've traveled the world. Today my daughter and I made large batches of jam and jars of pickled vegetables. We enjoy many of the same television shows and movies so usually spend our evenings watching together or we still read aloud or listen to audio books. Of course, we often travel for extended periods of time and so much of our day depends on our location. But even when traveling we have a flow and ease together with each person tending to take on various roles and tasks. We prefer slow travel and immersive learning rather than racing through tourist places. In fact, our most memorable trips have been about the local people we got to know rather than the landmarks seen. Our family get-togethers always include stories about "remember that guy who . . ." or "I still can't believe we met. . . ."

Worldschooling has allowed us to experience life in so many diverse cultures and to really see a multitude of perspectives and ways of living. Cultural immersion is such a rich part of how we live and learn that even our home-based times are filled with global foods, international media, and chats with friends around the world. And having been able to learn about our gloriously diverse world through self-directed/determined, immersive learning means it is real and internalized rather than simply being mandated to be accepting. I watch the grace and civility that my teens and young adults live by and I am so grateful that we have been able to experience and learn globally. All five have spent multiple times living in the Middle East and are comfortable with various religions and beliefs. They spent formative years hearing the call to prayer five times a day or not eating in public during Ramadan. Just as they were accepted by Muslim friends there, so they accept and embrace diversity now as adults. They are not afraid of difference but are curious and welcoming. These are attributes I think many of us wish more people in the world had!

Those acceptances of others and finding peace and comfort within our own relationships and home are aspects of our lives that I am so thankful for. I remember years ago people laughing at my big crowd of children and warning "just wait until they are all teens!" There was an ominous tone suggesting that we were going to be thrust into anger and door slamming with the shouting of "I hate you" constantly. After the first son navigated adolescence with ease, I thought it just a measure of his easy-going temperament. But then second, third, fourth, and now fifth child are demonstrating that life does not have to be lived with this level of negative drama.

But how have we escaped this and the ensuing stress? Well, I'm seeing so many headlines right now during the Covid-19 shut downs with things like "How to survive being trapped with your children all day," or "how to survive homeschooling your children," which makes me so sad. Sure, we can all remember days with infants and toddlers where we had dreams of running away to a place that wasn't sticky, no one's diaper needed changing, and we could sleep or use the bathroom in peace, but how sad if the days with our children always need "surviving" rather than embracing. The attachment parenting practices we adopted and our unschooling/worldschooling ideologies have led to the majority of our time together being relaxed and happy. We work as a team and if someone is experiencing a problem then everyone pulls together to help. This doesn't mean we have never had frustrations or worries about our lives—we are normal. But being together so much has meant we have learned how best to help each person in finding their individual path while knowing that they have a large group of cheerleaders behind them and a strong physical and emotional support structure.

Lev Vygotsky was a Russian psychologist who outlined the notion of scaffolding learning which is basically where someone who knows how to do something helps those who don't and gradually lessens the help as the person masters the task. Our family tends to do this with the process of moving into adulthood. The doors are always open so you can head out and try one path but if needed come back home and then take off in a new direction; all with scaffolds and supports from the home base. Looking back at my own life I always had that from my grandmother and mother which is why I developed the confidence to try new paths and take journeys into the unknown. From an attachment theory perspective, we call this a secure base. Knowing that we have a solid "home" base of help, allows us to be more independent in life. So, from parenting in ways that promoted security in attachment relationships, to trusting children's ability to self-direct/ determine their learning, and then giving that strong supportive foundation of love with freedom, meant that our family journey was one of increased joy and laughter and reduced stress and drama.

Connection to Work

In my own university teaching I read many articles and help my own students teach and counsel children who are growing up with a multitude of problems. The Adverse Childhood Experiences (ACEs) studies are just some of the vast research that show the incredible problems for so many of our world's children. It's heart breaking to think of youngsters growing up with this level of stress. But this stress is not only found in the more gruesome stories but in the day-to-day trauma that many children experience in traditional or "factory" education (so named as publics schools were started to provide a workforce of mediocrely educated individuals). For many children, schools are NOT a safe and comfortable place and there is little learning other than to fear the world. Parents are caught in a cycle of "it was okay for me so you will survive it too" mentality and don't know that we can break out of this and that children can learn freely, via self-direction/determination, and with joy. Our families *can be* safe places to nourish and help children grow emotionally and also allow them the space to learn and develop at their own pace and learn based on their interests.

We have so many tools available to us now with the advent of digital media and online learning and access to information. Hopefully parents who are perhaps transitioning to virtual work and children who are experiencing online learning with more down time and freedom of schedule during this Covid-19 situation, may obtain a glimpse into a different way to live. Wouldn't it be an amazing outcome of a horrible pandemic, if families are able to become closer and foster a different and healthier emotional path of relationships and learning. We can only hope.

References:

Kolb, D. A. (1984). *Experiential learning: Experience as the source of learning and development.* Englewood Cliffs: Prentice-Hall.

As a Family Education Consultant, **Dr. Kate Green** helps parents make decisions about their children's educational journey by using research-based strategies and information in combination with their intuitive inner voice to help understand what is optimum for their family.

She has guided educational decision making and learning for three decades now—working in the early childhood, elementary, and adolescence age groups to mentoring adults through doctoral degrees. She has five very successful, alternatively educated young adult and teen children of her own and loves to help other families make decisions that enable their children to joyfully excel.

Chapter 5

I Love Learning

Katy Burke

When I first discovered Princeton Learning Cooperative (PLC) as a high school teacher of thirteen years, I thought someone had pulled my dream straight out of my head and used it as a blueprint for a real, in-living-color place. It's no longer the fantasy I thought it was, but it is still wonderfully unique. As a public high school teacher, I dreamed of a school where kids learned by sitting around a table asking and answering thoughtful questions, where teachers knew not only their students but also their families, and where meaningful honest feedback replaced grades. I would face stacks of student papers and agonize over what number grade to slap on pages full of words. I wished I could just sit down with each kid and explain my thoughts as I read. I thought of a Rumi quote that a colleague had hanging on the wall of her classroom, "Out beyond ideas of wrongdoing and rightdoing there is a field. I'll meet you there." That's the relationship I wanted with my students, where I wasn't judge or manager or disciplinarian, but, teacher and mentor—that's all.

Princeton Learning Cooperative is that place. PLC is a full-time self-directed learning center for teens. The approach to learning here is simple . . . focus on the strengths and interests of the kid, each kid individually. In public school, students with learning differences might get an IEP, an Individualized Education Plan. Except it wasn't individualized at all. Nearly every plan listed the same accommodations:

preferential seating, extra time for tests and assignments, allowance to leave the classroom when needed, copies of the notes, etc. What makes PLC revolutionary is that everyone's learning is individualized, in its entirety. In a sense, everyone needs an "IEP." There are so many unique minds out there. The learning here isn't simply modified for individual kids, it's created BY them, for them, with the help of an invested adult, their mentor. And we always begin with a simple question: What do you want to learn?

You'd be surprised how many people don't have an answer to that question. They've never been asked it before. This question is foundational to sincere and lasting learning in young adults. Sure, there are times we learn things that we don't have interest in. I'm not a mechanically-minded person, but I certainly cared a lot about how to fix a flat tire when I got two. And there are times we discover what we want to learn by simply giving something a try, something seemingly unappealing. However, by and large, deep learning is born of an initial, genuine desire. So we start with the basics: What do you want to learn? As a former public school teacher, the profundity of this question is not lost on me. In a field in which the question historically, universally, has been, "What should they learn?," this new question is truly radical. It's loving. It's freeing. It opens up the world to young people at a point in their lives when they are most ripe for the adventure.

Of course, figuring out what they want to learn is half the journey. When teens first come to us, together we draw up a list of their interests and start looking for ways that they can learn more about those things.

Chapter 5

Sometimes we already have classes to accommodate them, but often we look for volunteers from the community to teach. There are some wonderfully generous and interesting people out there who want to share their knowledge and skills with young people. We have a retired New Jersey general assemblyman teaching a lively class on the judicial process; a Cambridge-educated psychiatrist living in the states with her family teaching well-loved classes on psychology; a music-writing, French-lit reading, math teacher, leading a role-playing games class; and nearly thirty more fascinating folks giving their time to help our kids find their way. The teens have diverse interests, and we have a diverse volunteer staff to show for it. Once, we had a young man confidently tell us that he wanted to learn metal forging and conversational Russian. Now that's a challenge. Surprisingly, there is a working blacksmith still in Trenton, who, lo and behold, spoke Russian! We helped to set up an internship, and it took off from there. It's not always that easy, though. Sometimes, we can't find a teacher, and we help the teen to learn independently. Often, the kids aren't so sure of what they want to learn, at least at first. They just start somewhere and navigate their way forward with the help of adult mentors and their own compass, which they are learning to read better all the time. If this sounds a little bit like the hero's journey, it is. Learning should be a journey to deeper understanding and a wiser self.

The Benefits of Self-Directed Learning

Katy Burke

After working in this environment for five years, I believe that the single greatest benefit to this educational approach is that the process of exploration inevitably leads to a security of self. Not every kid who leaves us is a fully mature adult. Most are not. However, they're on their way. They're further along than how they came to us, and not just in superficial ways, like how to take notes or study for a test. They are more self-aware, more self-controlled, more sure of themselves and where they're headed. They're braver. When I taught high school seniors in public school, I knew many young people who didn't know themselves. They might as well have been picking colleges and majors out of a hat. They would have benefitted from a different choice, a gap year, some life experience. There were a handful, however, that I just knew were going to be okay. My assurance wasn't contingent on their grades or work habits, but an observable sense of security that each possessed. At PLC, that feeling is the norm when a young person moves on from us. I believe that is because they are given room to breathe, to dream and to try.

The environment at PLC is, well, as changeable as an adolescent. It can shift from drowsy to dramatic in an instant. Usually, it's somewhere in between. Teenagers get a bad rap, but they are actually really fun people! They're old enough to make witty jokes and young enough to still live in the present. They relish each new experience like a flavor they've never tasted before. They're both fragile and daring at the same time. So you can imagine what it would be like with about thirty of these individuals in the same space. Never dull and messy in every way. I say that endearingly. Here we let the mess occur, then we help *them* clean it up, whether it be a bunch of shavings left on the floor from wood carving, a rude remark to another teen or a late arrival to a tutoring session. Yet, beneath the messiness, there is a real sense of peace because here there are no external pressures to grow up faster or be someone you're not. There is no pseudo-academic tone to "be in the know" and "on track." It is in this kind of authentic environment that young people can catch their breath, really learn what interests them, and find their way. Eventually, they thrive.

Many of our members are coming to us from public school. The time and freedom afforded here is completely foreign to them. For many, but not all, the opportunity to catch their breath, means months of what we have termed "deschooling." Those months are precious. It's time for these kids to peel off, shake off, or sleep off all of the stress, anxiety, and sometimes, shame, that they have brought with them. It's as if they have left their twenty pound bookbag at the door, but still carry all that phantom weight on their backs. If they are allowed space and time without interference, they come around . . . lighter, in fact.

Stories of our Students

When Sam came to us, he spent his first two months lying in a beanbag chair, wearing headphones, listening to music. One day, out of the blue really, he announced he wanted to go to college and needed to know how to do that. Before we knew it, he was attending classes, doing outside work, then leading classes, working an internship, working his own DJ business, speaking on a panel for teen entrepreneurs, speaking at a local town council meeting and much more. Now he's going to school for communications and working a fabulous internship with the New Jersey Department of Education. It's interesting how things come around.

Sawyer struggled with anxiety, fear, and insomnia. But Sawyer is a natural born artist and a creative mind. Now in his second year at PLC, he has elaborate ongoing artistic projects, most of which he is doing completely on his own from start to finish: themed photography shoots, dance routines, fabric art, special effects makeup, stained glass, drawing, painting, short film, and sewing projects. Currently, he is sewing a six-foot Sandworm from the *Beetlejuice* movie . . . you know, just for fun. He also does the backstage lighting for many local theater shows.

Ryan had a slow start when he came to us. He was burnt out from school and would often miss days at PLC. But slow and steady wins the race. Eventually, Ryan was not only coming in consistently, but he was the member most committed to his classes. He also used much of his spare time to work through an accounting textbook. He thinks logically and works efficiently. He started community college early and breezed through the accounting classes, much of which he had already taught himself.

Self-Determined Learning

Chapter 5

That is what this kind of learning looks like. It looks a lot like taking responsibility, rather, *choosing* responsibility. It looks a lot like becoming an adult. And isn't that what we want? To help kids grow into free-thinking responsible adults? Notice that the kids didn't come to us that way. Neither did we mold them that way. We simply offered the right environment, opportunity, feedback, and support, and they *chose* that way. Still, sometimes they don't, at least not for some time. Disengagement is always a possibility because another component to this approach is that learning is non-compulsory.

Part of the ease of our environment is that the adults aren't spending the day telling the teens what to do. Teens are free to opt out of any given learning experience, whether it be a class, a trip, a work opportunity, etc. They may spend most of the day sleeping on the couch if they so choose, or the bean bag chair. This may seem like a completely terrible education plan, but it is the axis upon which thriving independent young adults spin. I remember an early conversation I had with Joel Hammon, co-founder of PLC, in which he explained one of his first experiences in the center. Only a handful of boys were members at the time and on one particular day, they all chose to spend the entire day goofing off and playing video games. As he tells it, his initial reaction was, "Good God, what have I done?" Are teenagers really capable of consistently making good choices about how they spend their time?

The short answer is, no. I mean, are most adults capable of consistently making good choices about how they spend their time? I can tell you from personal observation that Joel Hammon may be, but I think he's an exception. So then aren't we setting kids up to fail? No, we are setting them up to succeed. They learn how to do well by first "messing up." My secret pet name for self-directed education is free-will education. In all honesty, I don't care for the term "self-directed" because I don't think learning (or life, for that matter) is something we direct, but we are capable of making decisions that produce real results, for good or for bad. Recall the Judeo-Christian story of the fall of man. Adam and Eve were told not to eat of the Tree of Knowledge of Good and Evil. Yet, they *could* if they chose to for they were given free-will. So why was the tree there in the first place? Why offer the option to fail? Because without the ability to choose the wrong way, they are robbed of the *ability to choose* the right way. There is no free-will. Why does PLC offer the option to waste time, to miss opportunities? Because without it, young people don't have the option to make good choices with their time. They can only comply with or rebel against another's direction. In a constant state of compliance, how would they ever feel a sense of control? And without a sense of control, how would they ever become internally motivated or take ownership of their lives?

In an interview with Stephen Dubner of Freakonomics Radio, Charles Duhigg, author of *Better, Smarter, Faster: The Transformative Power of Real Productivity,* explains that after talking to several hundred highly successful people about motivation, he discovered the most powerful common denominator among them is a solid sense of control. He says, "We trigger self-motivation by making choices that make us feel in control. The act of asserting ourselves and taking control helps trigger the parts of our neurology where self-motivation resides." So, at PLC we ask the kids "What do you want to learn?" and then offer them a precious resource to steward however they *choose*: time.

Teens and Time

In my mind, there is no gift more valuable than that of time. Teens are transitioning to adulthood, but they're not there yet. Therefore, their time is truly free. For adults, time is money, for kids, it's a resource in itself. How different would our adult lives be if we learned the value of time before we found ourselves forever at its heels? I think our relationship with time would be much healthier. We would likely be more intentional with it rather than playing catch up, and through intention we would discover our priorities. This is exactly what happens at PLC. The kids choose what they want to learn, when they want to learn, and how they want to learn. They may choose to spend their time learning one or two things very deeply or jump around learning a bunch of different things. They may choose to learn in a class, with a tutor, on the job, through self-study, with books or videos or by self-creation. Even in a classroom setting, the kids make choices all the time. Usually they all sit facing each other around a table and talk. With the teacher and one another, they sometimes talk about what to learn next. Essentially, they learn how to make choices by *choosing*.

This learning process, however, is not without struggle. Though we value choice over compulsion, commitments are still respected, and there are natural consequences for not keeping them. We are learner-centered, but that doesn't mean that learners' choices happen in a bubble. No, they happen in a community of other learners, volunteer teachers, and mentors. Therefore, if a teen makes a choice to be part of a class and then fails to show consistently, the class suffers, and the teen misses out on learning. If a teen chooses not to keep a commitment to a tutor, that volunteer may choose to discontinue the arrangement, or we, as a staff, may bring it to a close. We do make apologies on the behalf of kids who are struggling to keep commitments, but we won't do that forever. There are natural consequences. It is our hope, though, that when teens realize they want to discontinue with classes or tutors, they will come to those decisions thoughtfully and inform their volunteers ahead of time. As mentors, we coach them to do this. This process can be just as valuable a learning experience as the class itself. However, because they're still learning, they don't always do things thoughtfully or responsibly. When that happens, time is the best teacher.

I worked with a young man in his final year here at PLC. In his last couple of months, he expressed regret for failing to take his math tutoring sessions seriously. They ended prematurely, and, at the time, he didn't have any desire to pick it back up. In retrospect, he felt differently. In his own words, he "missed an opportunity." That may sound a bit tragic, but we don't think so. He learned something with a farther-reaching application than polynomials: willingness. An attitude of willingness, rather than willfulness or apathy, is pivotal in becoming a lifelong learner. From this lesson, he can approach future learning opportunities with an "I get to" rather than an "I have to" or "I don't have to" mindset. He also is not barred forevermore from learning math. We've found that kids can learn a great deal of math, writing or whatever it may be, rather easily when they've come around to the idea of it on their own. There is no shortage of resources to do so.

Acceptance and Support

The environment at PLC is low pressure and unintimidating. Genuine learning is born out of curiosity, and it's nearly impossible to sustain a state of curiosity while simultaneously living in a state of anxiety. Therefore, we aim to understand, support, and even extend some grace. However, when the external pressures are lifted, undergirding it, is an authentic internal itch to do something of value. Motivation. We all feel it eventually. There's nothing wrong with external motivation per se, but when you strip away grades, requirements, and deadlines, a pressure from below, the pressure not to waste our time, rises to the surface. For a lot of kids, this takes a while. They may still be feeling residual compulsory pressure from their time in school, or they may just be relishing in their newfound freedom. Both of these phases fall under "deschooling," the process by which a former student of traditional school shifts their mindset from "have to" to "get to." However, like the young man who regretted a missed opportunity, kids eventually feel that healthy internal pressure bubbling up, especially as they see their friends maturing around them. I believe that people want to offer something of value. If that's not the case, it signifies dysfunction. Internal or external, something is getting in the way. Sometimes, the something that inhibits the desire to learn, is school.

Internal Motivation

Nearly every parent and teacher wants their kids to be internally motivated. To that end, we brainstorm ways to spark their interest or instill in them a sense of responsibility. The aim is to create or inject internal motivation. However, that's a tad oxymoronic, isn't it? Internal motivation, by nature, is present, albeit latent, in all of us. What's needed is the removal of arbitrary external motivators that cloud a person's internal drive or prevent it from kicking into gear. The fewer perfunctory duties imposed, the more room for meaningful choices. Not simply choices to chase fun, but choices to take on fulfilling responsibilities. Decision-making is fundamental in taking ownership over one's education, and it's also a natural part of adolescence when kids instinctively seek independence. This does not mean, however, that we leave kids floundering on their own. Being internally motivated and self-sufficient often get lumped together, but they occur quite differently. The former, I believe, happens naturally under the right conditions; the latter takes some work and usually some communal support. While being independent, by definition, is a solo act; *becoming* independent is often a cooperative effort.

Perhaps PLC and centers like ours, should call ourselves "*Becoming* Self-Directed Learning Centers" instead of "Self-Directed Learning Centers," because when a child truly becomes secure, confident and experienced in their learning, that's usually when they move on from us. We've done our work. The staff, as mentors, help teens to need us less. It's a strange business model for sure, but it's what they need. "Self-directed education" means different things to different people. I've heard public school educators use it to mean giving kids more choice about what they learn in the classroom, but because this is still within a required curriculum and a fixed system of external motivation (grading), it does not qualify as self-directed by the standards of the self-directed learning (SDL)community. Others think of self-directed as synonymous with self-determined education in which kids are not only learning in their own way, but they are learning *how* to find their way. In this approach, there is a focus on growth mindset and a real sense of autonomy. This is very much our hope for kids at PLC. Autonomy, that's the goal. The method, however, is to cooperate in mentoring relationships with the kids in pursuit of that goal. Without ever disregarding their power of choice, we help them to reflect and move through the learning-to-learn process until they're, as we put it, "driving the bus."

The Role of a Mentor

Katy Burke

Mentoring requires a delicate balance of involvement and disengagement. It's analogous to teaching someone to drive, except the teens are learning to drive their lives, not cars. This is where the work gets hard. First, you find yourself in the driver's seat asking them where to go. No, that's wrong; first, you find yourself waiting for the teen to simply get in the car. While some kids are restless to start right away, others take many many months. That's often the "deschooling" process mentioned before. *Then* you're driving for a bit, just modeling and taking input from them. Eventually, they're in the driver's seat. You hold back quite a bit, but, still, you provide needed feedback along the way. Further down the road, they're pretty much driving on their own, and you're just there to enhance the experience, to offer some useful tips and keep them company as they gain confidence in their abilities. Finally, you're out of the car and at home calling them to pick up milk from the store. Okay, maybe that last bit of the analogy doesn't quite work for our purposes. Though we do call on former PLC members to speak at events and to teach classes. It's tough getting there though. It's tough to know *when* to hold back. It's tough actually holding back, and it's tough giving feedback subtly, skillfully, so that teens will listen and not withdraw. But this *is* the work, and again it's what teenagers *need* to really grow into their own. They need a lot of space and caring, attentive adults on stand-by. Of course, it depends on the kid, but if mentoring is done well, the teen feels both free and supported. That's the balance.

So what does this look like in reality? Every teen at our center has a staff mentor that they meet with once a week for about an hour. For some kids, an hour is too long, so we meet for half the time. Mentoring meetings can really vary depending on the person. Some teens are more academically focused. We talk about what they're learning, what they want to learn, how to do that, and together we document their learning to prepare for college applications down the road. We talk about documentaries they watched, books they're reading, day trips or volunteering experiences that they might undertake. Other teens are more interested in doing their own thing than pursuing academic goals, whether that something is artistic, mechanical, or technical in nature. They share what they're doing, and we help them to reflect on their work experiences and the new skills they're learning. With their consent, we help to hold them accountable for meeting short term goals, and we help them find new opportunities. Other kids work on personal matters: forming or breaking habits, making friendships, finding their voice, etc. We spend a lot of time in conversation about their social and/or emotional lives, their well-being, and healthy practices. Many teens struggle with getting enough sleep, so we work on that if they desire. Often mentoring meetings are a combination of these approaches. They decide how we use our time and what they're working towards.

The beauty of this process is that every kid has at least one grown person who is on their side *and* not their parent. That is incredibly valuable to a young person's maturation and independence because they're in the process of separating themselves from their parents but still in need (and often in want!) of adult support. In the traditional school system, where kids are grouped with hundreds of direct peers and number thirty to one teacher per classroom, adult-teen collaboration is hardly possible. For us, it's the cornerstone of what we do. Therefore, in addition to all the reflection and planning that goes on in mentoring meetings, we spend a lot of time just building relationships, really getting to know the teens. They start to trust us and share more of themselves, which helps us to provide more authentic and relevant support. We are there to encourage them in their small steps forward, which are not necessarily academic accomplishments, such as an "A" on the vocabulary test. Instead, it might be the first time we see a kid initiate an apology to a peer or when a particularly shy kid tells a joke in front of a group. These things are small in action, but big in personal growth. On the academic side of things, we provide meaningful feedback rather than grades. I still work with kids on their writing, but, just as I had always hoped, I now sit next to them and talk with the kids as I read their work. I share my reactions, impressions, any confusion, and they clarify what they had in mind. Except for some obvious grammatical errors, it's not about right or wrong, but about communication, exactly as writing should be. As mentors, we guide, encourage and collaborate.

The Power of Community

Beyond the freedom, time, and adult support, we offer teens and their families a community. Community, I believe, is the last crucial element in this educational approach. Kids need not only the support of friendly adults, but friendship with other kids. They need both a strong sense of individual identity and a sense of belonging. From my experience, those who have a hard time with either, usually have a hard time pursuing learning. Culturally, there is a belief that when kids get together they distract each other from their studies. Though I don't argue that this is sometimes true, it is *also* true that a strong foundation for learning is simply having a core group of friends. Having friends is a need we all have, and it can't be ignored, regardless of how much of a loner or rebel a particular teen may be. If this need is met, it often breeds a zest for life *and learning.* Therefore, we encourage lots of social interaction at our center, we talk about the current culture of the group at our staff meetings, and we support activities, such as purely fun day trips, in order to build community. We also value building relationships with parents and providing a community for them. I remember my first "parent conference" as a staff member at PLC. It was on a street corner in Trenton with a parent who ran a coffee business from a bicycle cart. It was a great conversation and unbelievably good coffee. We care about parents, and how they are doing. We host family picnics, hikes and get-togethers for parents to discuss their parenting struggles, and we even provide beer and wine at our version of back-to-school night. Oh my! At PLC, we recognize that like most endeavors, learning happens best through connection and collaboration.

Community doesn't just serve as a feel-good motivator. For the kids, it has a very practical purpose. Without it, learners will not see the real-life application and utility of their studies. Our kids sometimes have fun chasing informational rabbit holes to see where they lead. They routinely share facts and ideas with me that I hadn't known previously. There's the rub . . . the sharing. That's where the rubber meets the road, where a teen can see how their newly developed ideas, acquired information, or skills, are received by others. We don't live in a bubble, so there is no point learning in one. Not only is there quite a bit of sharing going on, but we have a good number of kids who teach classes themselves. This is a test of the strength, utility and mastery of the information they've acquired. How well do you know your stuff? Do other people find it helpful? I think this is a far greater measurement of one's skill and knowledge than a typical exam. Kids are actually interacting with the material while aiding others in interacting with it. That is true preparation for becoming a contributing member of society. Community is not only helpful, it's crucial.

The approach of PLC and our sister centers is straightforward in concept. We provide learners with the freedom to make their own choices, the time to learn and grow at their own pace, plentiful opportunities and resources (including a large group of fascinating volunteer teachers), mentoring support with caring adults, and a community in which to belong. This is simple but not easy. There are days when the messiness of the work is overwhelming, but there is meaning and purpose in it. It sure beats trying to untangle senseless bureaucratic knots. Also, the messiness validates the aim. Because the work is challenging, I know we're affecting real change. If the kids were already grown and put together, they wouldn't need us. Again, that's the goal. Boiled down, the work of education is helping

young people put themselves and their lives
together. I'm happy to spend my days doing that.

Katy Burke has worked with teens her entire career as a
public school teacher, but PLC allows her to be much
more involved in their lives. She loves getting to know
the whole person; working, playing, and laughing
alongside them; giving them comfort and counsel when
needed; and developing relationships with the teens'
families. When not working, she is raising 2 daughters,
managing her home, getting involved in her church and
local community, and learning more about topics she
personally finds meaningful.

Our Journey into Learning—We Are Worldschoolers

Laine Liberti

Three things you need to know right up front. 1) I make lists 2) I research everything ad nauseam and 3) I ask a lot of questions.

I'm a list maker. I make lists that cover to do's, goals, things I want to learn, people I admire, ideas, ethics. This tool has always been helpful to me in order to weigh out big decisions, provide organization of big ideas and help me make sense of my learning.

In addition to making lists, I am an amateur researcher of all things that catch my interest. My research includes lots of reading, watching videos, listening to podcasts and asking questions. In fact, I ask a lot of questions to anyone who will give my questions attention, to anyone not put off by my incessant curiosity, to anyone receptive of my state of ever-consistent inquiry. This type of curiosity has served me well in my former professional life, where I conducted market research, focus groups and interviewed thousands of people over the past two decades. It has served me well as I travel down the path of a self-directed/determined learner. Much of what I share here in this chapter started from lists, then researched both internally and externally and finally expressed through questions and answers. Welcome to my mind.

A Brief History

Chapter 6

I'm a single mother to a self-actualized learner named Miro.

From an educational standpoint, Miro's journey into self-directed learning finds its roots in the conventional American public school system. Miro's early education included a combination of Montessori and public schooling until he became a fifth grade dropout.

In the early days, my thinking was pretty conventional surrounding education. I had always believed it was someone else's job to educate my child and that I was not qualified. I was a business owner, my specialty was marketing, branding, and advertising and I knew nothing at all about "education." There were experts for that sort of thing.

Miro has a quick mind. When he was in the public school system, he often finished his class work quickly as the lessons were far below his current learning level. Miro found himself bored in school, resentful of being asked to perform basic reading comprehension tasks. Equally annoying was the persistent requirement to fill in the blanks, color between the lines, conform and regurgitate.

At the time, I believed school was important. School was the place where one receives an "education" and I agreed, my son **must be educated**. I believed that standardized education was the great equalizer and that only through "education" my son would be prepared for his future success. I also believed the purpose of education was to prepare all children to be good citizens and good workers. Looking back, I find it strange that I had never considered that I was a self-taught branding expert and propelled my career into success through my own interests, self-directed learning and professional inquiry and not the result of my own standardized education.

In my professional life, my success translated into a full workload, often requiring 12 to 14 hour work days. As a single mom and a business owner of a successful marketing and branding agency, I felt countless pressures at all times. My relationship with Miro paid the heaviest price. I rationalized that I had no choice; I was building a future for us, living the American Dream. In reality, I spent very little time with my son who often chanted his pleading mantra, "Mom, you never spend any time with me. You are always working." Each time I heard his truth, my heart broke into a million tiny pieces. Still, I believed there was no other option.

Early 2008, the California economy crashed. By December of the same year, it became clear that I would need to close my agency. The financial pressures increased, stresses compounded, and I knew that I would not be bringing my staff back in the following January.

Late one night, I sat in the office with my then 9-year-old son Miro, who was engrossed in his video game. I glanced up at him, no longer focused on the end-of-year accounting. Without hesitation I said, "Miro, let's get rid of everything, sell all this stuff, and let's go have an adventure! We can get backpacks, travel through Latin America, and explore whatever we wish."

Also without hesitation, Miro replied, "I'm in!"

We planned, sold, consolidated, and gave all of our things away in preparation for our journey. In less

Chapter 6

than six months our plan came to fruition. Our intention was to backpack from North America, into Central and South America, letting inspiration be our guide. We planned on finishing our adventure in Ushuaia, the southernmost tip of Argentina.

Intuitively I knew Miro would learn by encountering all the unique cultures we were going to travel through, living history and exploring archaeology in person. I knew we'd be exposed to geography and see first-hand the planet's ecology through the lens of science. I knew my son would be exposed to practical math through money conversions and budgets, calculating time zones and distances as we navigated the continents. I knew we'd learn some Spanish and be exposed to countless other unexpected wonders. I knew that in one year of travel, we'd experience deep, rich learning that fifth grade could never provide.

I wasn't worried about Miro's education then, because the thought that always followed in my head was he'll head back to school when we return and pick up where he left off. However, I often felt cognitive dissidence surrounding my attitudes and beliefs about education. But I set that aside to have an adventure with Miro, dedicated to a time of clearing, healing, and being together.

How will I educate your Miro?

Miro and I were about eight months into our travels, we recognized that there was no urgency for us to return to our conventional lives back in the States. Together, we decided to continue on our path of travel

101

indefinitely. That marked the point I started to research, make lists, ask questions and learn everything I could about education, learning modalities and learning alternatives in order to come up with a plan for my son's education.

Through my research, I discovered there was an active alternative education movement that I had never heard of. First, I read the works of John Holt, Ivan Illich, John Taylor Gatto, Alfie Kohn, and A.S Neill. I read blogs, explored homeschooling modalities, participated in online discussion groups and watched videos of Astra Taylor and others sharing their own learning journeys. I researched the brain and the biology of learning.

Unschooling

I was engrossed in all of it wondering why hadn't I focused my attention to these topics before? I made lists, lots of lists about our options, weighed the pros and cons and started to ask questions to understand the mechanics deeper. But I always came back to "unschooling," a philosophy that resonated deeply.

> There is no one way to unschool. Unschooling is primarily about process not content. The process of learning, the process of knowing yourself, openness, confidence, self-determination, independent thinking, critical thinking . . . none of which one gets when following other people's agenda. Making one's own agenda is what it is all about. This is done not in isolation but in the

context of one's family and community (Joel Hawthorne, 2011).

Unschooling is a term that the late John Holt coined in the 1970s to describe learning that is based on a child's interests and needs. Unschooling does not begin with a parent's notion of what is important to learn and then turn the choices of how to learn the content over to a child. Rather, it begins with the child's natural curiosity and expands from there. Unschooling is not "instruction free" learning. If a child wants to learn to read, an unschooling parent may offer instruction by providing help with decoding, reading to the child, and giving the child ample opportunity to encounter words. If the child is uninterested in these supports, the parent backs off until the child asks for help. The most important thing about the unschooling process is that the child is in charge of the learning, not the adult. Unschoolers often do no traditional school work, yet they do learn traditional subject matter. They learn it as a natural extension of exploring their own personal interests.

The more I researched the more my ideas about education expanded. I resonated with the philosophy of unschooling movement, and the concept of self-directed learning came alive for us. Learning more about unschooling gave me the language to frame the learning we were already doing. Through that lens, I realized that not only was Miro learning so much from the world around him, and I had witnessed him grow leaps and bounds in just the eight months we had been traveling at that point.

Excitedly, I shared my discovery with Miro. We talked about learning and education and agreed we were now officially "unschoolers." Voila! Now that we had language to call it we would now bring intentionality into our natural learning process.

Miro pointed out to me that I was always asking questions, so I never really stopped being a learner (even though I was an adult) and I was actually already an unschooler! This realization felt empowering to me and gave me permission to become a "learner" once again. My fears about not being qualified to "teach my son" were quieted and I approached learning with the full force of my natural curiosity. Miro noticed this too.

From that point forward, Miro and I committed to extending our agreement about partnership in budget and travel matters into our learning journey as well. And yes, I agreed to be accountable for following my interests too. This agreement brought us into a non-hierarchical approach to learning and education. We agreed to support each other's interests, show up for each other's learning, and both engage as learner and facilitator.

For the first several years of our "uschooling journey" I facilitated Miro by learning alongside him based on his interests. As he grew older, he modeled the same behavior for me.

Living in an age where information is available at our fingertips and we didn't find a lack of resources, even on the road. The world around us, combined with our natural curiosity provided an ample classroom to learn. We used inquiry, research, and personal experiences as our guides. Daily we were prompted to ask "why," "how," "who," or even "when." But we soon discovered that asking "why" was the most powerful question among those. Anything that we wished to learn, we could by just seeking answers to those questions we had could dive in deeper.

What is Worldschooling?

Worldschooling is the intentional act of viewing the world as one's classroom. Sounds similar to the unschooling definition above. Yes, it's true, but there is one clear distinction for us. We've combined unschooling with a lifestyle of travel and exploration.

In its simplest form, worldschooling is the act of combining education and travel usually led through experiential learning and inquiry. Worldschooling takes the principles of learning outside of a classroom, combining family multi-age learning with travel, utilizing cultural and social learning as the foundation. The other quality unique to worldschooling is utilizing worldviews as a lens to consider global perspectives and explore how we fit into the world.

The term "Worldschooling" was coined over a decade ago and has been used by thousands of families since. Miro and I have helped to popularize the term through our work, community building and advocacy. Worldschooling has become a broad educational philosophy that combines each individual family's educational style with some level of travel. What makes worldschooling different from other educational modalities, is that there is no one way to worldschool. For example, my family's brand of worldschooling combines self-directed inquiry, unschooling, social and experiential learning, and travel. Others may include a formal homeschool curriculum. Others yet may travel part time and enroll their kids into a local school for the cultural immersive experience. There are as many ways to worldschool as there are families.

However, what all worldschoolers do have in common is the desire to adapt worldly experiences as inspiration to learn and go deeper. Worldschooling provides a "world-class education" to all that are faced with the demands of a highly globalized and changing world.

What Worldschooling Looks Like

I am always surprised when people want to see the results of our learning as I'm often asked to "prove" that my son is actually educated and has learned specific content. (Are schooled children subjected to the same line of questioning?)

At this point, we have the luxury of looking over the last eleven years of travel, conversations, explorations, and experiences to be able to respond to questions as a cumulative body of experiences, often making our answers rich and textured. As Miro and I are at the forefront of the worldschooling movement, we try to field these questions with as much grace as possible. I thought it would be a wonderful example to share how we respond to some of these questions.

In an interview for a Slovakian newspaper, Miro and I were asked a question about how he (we) learned about World War II without ever going to school. Fortunately, this was a topic we have explored in some detail over the years, had many conversations and contextualized our experiences to create a larger understanding of the topic. Plus, I made lists. Here's our response:

> We first started our dive into the subject when we were living in a small beach town in Peru in 2011. We met a traveler in his early seventies and spent the entire afternoon with him listening to his stories about growing up near the Black Forest in Alsace (a historical region that has belonged to both Germany and France over the years) and his experiences during World War II as a young boy.
>
> He recanted his memories watching his world change as the war broke out around him. He shared feelings of shame making the choice as a young boy to join Hitler Youth in order to avoid being shipped off to a "punishment camp." The old man had been around Miro's age at the time and his memories were impactful on both of us. We learned about this man's life in the village during the war. He shared the fear of dying as his mom dug him out of the rubble after the building he was taking a piano lesson was bombed. He talked about his piano teacher being killed and how he remembers her face every time he sits down in front of a piano.
>
> His stories were real and his human experience prompted us to consider the human

toll, even from the point of view of a young Nazi. Later Miro and I learned more about the history of the Alsace, their role in the war, and considered this man's unique perspective from that point forward. We realized that history could never be told from one point of view that many perspectives make up the whole.

Years later, Miro and I hosted a retreat in Japan and listened to the perspectives of Japanese nationals who shared their family stories. One particular story had a strong effect on our understanding of World War II from the Japanese perspective. Our retreat partner was a woman about my age, who shared a story about her great uncle who was forced to become a kamikaze pilot for the Emperor in WWII. Her great uncle was short in stature which was the perfect physique to man a Kamikaze bomber, a plane equipped without an engine. Without a choice, the young man perished for his Emperor as many young men had. Our partner spoke about her great uncle with great reverence for his life and sacrifice and reflected that she might not be here with us, had her grandfather not been tall.

His story had been memorialized in her family's history, her understanding of her country's history, and the role and sacrifice her family made. We visited many war memorials and talked about the atrocities from the Japanese perspective about the bombs the US dropped in Hiroshima and Nagasaki. The human toll is incomprehensible.

Chapter 6

In Holland, our exploration through World War II continued after visiting the Anne Frank House and Museum. We looked at life through Anne Frank's eyes and imagined what her life must have been like. Together, Miro and I spoke in great detail about growing up Jewish under occupation and the cost of war on humanity. Simply reading Anne Frank's diary would have had a different effect on us. We were transported into the location that she was writing about and because of the sights and sounds, her words came alive. Anne Frank wrote, "I don't think of all the misery, but of the beauty that still remains." Together, Miro and I wondered, how she must have felt, what strength she must have drawn upon to have written that in her diary. Further, we wondered if we were capable of doing the same. Our experience was powerful and created the unexpected opportunity into a worldview that remains with us to this day.

In Budapest, we learned about the 20,000 Jews who were killed by the fascist Arrow Cross militiamen along the banks of the Danube, now memorialized by the bronze shoes along the river. Learning about their murders, standing and looking into the river, one can imagine a different time and actually feel the terror they must have felt. Another harrowing discovery Miro and I made was seeing the hundreds of "stumbling blocks" placed in front of homes where Jews lived throughout the city of Budapest. Each of these brass plates were engraved with the names of Holocaust victims, their date of birth, year of deportation, and cause of death.

Finally, in Poland, Miro and I researched the invasion of the country, the flashpoint kicking into World War II. We toured the Jewish ghettos of Warsaw & Krakow, walked through the rebuilt cities and dove deep into the country's rich history. We explored the uprising movement, emblematic of the spirit of human resilience. We learned about Poland's underground resistance fought by priests, citizens, teachers, and the Soviets who later became occupiers. We looked at the human cost from so many perspectives. Finally, with a heavy heart, Miro and I toured the extermination camps of Auschwitz and Birkenau, stood in the gas chambers where countless Jews lost their lives and learned about the inhumane acts that should never be replicated.

Our understanding of World War II may not be complete, but it's a deep experiential knowledge that has meaning to us through the places we've been, the experiences we've had, the people we've met and the stories we've heard.

But World War II wasn't the only conflict we've learned about. In Vietnam, we visited the Hỏa Lò Prison, where the French colonists in French Indochina jailed political prisoners, and later the North Vietnamese kept U.S. prisoners of war during the US / Vietnam War.

Chapter 6

In Cambodia, Miro walked through the famous Khmer Rouge Killing Fields. (I could not.)

In Nicaragua, where we lived for several months, we explored the recent history of the Nicaraguan Revolution, still fresh to the people's memories. In Managua, the capital where the Sandinistas ousted the Somoza dictatorship, we explored USA's political involvement through conversations, monuments, written history and more.

In Guatemala, we studied the genocide through the eyes of the indigenous Mayans still living in small communities surrounding Lake Atitlan. We explored the political rhetoric in the country's capital, examining history from several points of view. We participated in art happenings, exhibits, poetry readings and rallies as the human rights activist fought to keep the memories of those slain and disappeared alive. The genocide officially ended as recently as 1996, and even though Miro was born three years after, it became part of our lives too.

In South Africa, we visited the site that sparked the Soweto Uprising, standing on the corner where 12-year-old schoolboy Hector Pieterson was shot and killed. We visited the house where Nelson Mandela lived and examined the rise and fall of apartheid at The Apartheid Museum.

In Peru, we visited the places where the Inca Empire once thrived and eventually fell.

In Greece, we walked the path of the Gods, and visited the site of the Greco-Persian wars that took place in the 5th century BC.

In addition to the numerous wars we've investigated, we've equally explored cultures during times of peace throughout the ages, sparking art, music, literature, innovation and science.

The places themselves do not teach, rather it's the combination of research, inquiry, conversation, and exploration. As participants, we are actively engaged in the learning at all times. This context creates a personal relationship to what we are learning by weaving our own humanity throughout. We have become part of the story too, and this creates a personal responsibility to the future we wish to create.

The Purpose of Education

A big part of our journey into learning centered around redefining what education means to us. As soon as we replaced the word "education" with the word "learning" the world transformed into our greatest learning environment.

The other significant redefinition we found necessary was to expound the purpose of education. As you may conclude, I no longer believe standardized education is the great equalizer. Nor do I believe that the purpose of education is to produce good citizens. I believe the purpose of education is to develop a deep relationship to learning, even "a love of learning" which creates an empowered learner with agency, able to make choices about one's own learning (and life). That is my gift to my son. That is my gift to myself.

Eleven Compelling Reasons to Consider Worldschooling

I could not conclude my chapter in good conscience without first contributing a list. Often, those addressing education are looking solely at academic learning. I'd like to consider the other side of education commonly referred to as the "soft skills." If you still aren't convinced that worldschooling provides a world class education, I leave you with eleven compelling reasons to expand your thinking.

Educational Autonomy—As worldschoolers we combine the world around us with our own interest creating a direction or directions we wish to explore deeper. Through inquiry, exploration and research each worldschooler views the world through the lens of their own interests. For example, while a family may be exploring Paris together, each family member has the autonomy to go deeper based on their individual interests, creating layered experiential learning in the same location. One family member may focus on the history of Paris, the French Revolution and the changes the city took under Napoleon's rule. Another family member may be interested in looking deeper at the world of fashion and Coco Chanel's contribution to the world. And another family member may be interested in exploring the world of art and architecture by exploring

Art Nouveau and wandering through the multiple halls of the La Louve. Through worldschooling, the learner becomes responsible for directing their inquiry leading to deeper explorations and the family's role is to facilitate and learn in partnership with each member.

Learn Through Intrinsic Motivation—While there isn't anything required of worldschoolers other than to be present and intentional on their travels, the willingness to pursue a specific line of inquiry comes from their own intrinsic motivation. By being encouraged to tap into their own curiosity about the world around them, the excitement for learning comes from within. Being comfortable with pursuing one's own interest fueled by intrinsic motivation translates into a life-long love of learning.

Exercise Self-Advocacy & Self-Care—It is impossible to "show up" when our needs aren't being met. It is important to be aware of our own self-care, especially when we are traveling as often travel can create another level of stress and those around us surely feel it. Worldschooling encourages everyone to advocate for their own wellbeing and speak up for their own personal needs while also considering the needs of others. Through this, it's easier to create a balance between the needs of self, and the needs of the community or family.

Through this process, we can practice speaking up for ourselves and for others, developing strong communication skills, avoiding burnout and managing our time and energy more efficiently. This awareness will benefit anyone within any kind of group setting, whether it's family, personal, or professional.

Practice Teamwork—As parents, we say "your opinion matters." But children's voices are often quieted in conventional life, as routines, schedules, and responsibilities take a priority. However, traveling provides the perfect platform to empower all voices to be heard and to create equity among the family or group. Practicing group dynamics is one of the most important life lessons, and as worldschoolers become practiced in advocating for their own needs, they gain experience in compassion when others do the same. Through consciously focusing on what is best for the self and group, every voice is heard and each person has the responsibility to practice teamwork through compassion, compromise, negotiation, and leadership.

Be Adaptable—When you travel, things ultimately go wrong. There is no avoiding it, things get lost, there are unexpected weather conditions, issues come up surrounding transportation and unscheduled closures. Being able to adapt or make do is an important lesson in flexibility and adaptability. Those that practice letting go of expectations and going with the flow, add the important skill of adaptability and flexibility to their list of mastery.

Develop Grit—Employers often search for candidates who have grit, but how does one develop it? Worldschooling offers the opportunity to practice perseverance, which is at the foundation of developing

"grit." Worldschooling relies on the ability to show up, be accountable for one's own learning, and the ability to move through challenges and to persevere in the face of challenges.
Worldschooling and travel provide the perfect combination to do just that.

Practice Real World Problem Solving—Through travel, worldschoolers have the opportunity to make real-world decisions, solve problems in context, plan and manage budgets. Learners of all ages have the opportunity to be engaged in decisions like location selection, researching itineraries, logistics, budget, rentals, transportation, history and so much more. Often, challenges arise, and solutions must be decided upon. Having the opportunity to be involved in that process from all ages creates a skillset that will be with you for life.

Build Worldly Social Skills—As you can imagine, worldschooling provides the platform to interact with people from around the world. Through my son's eleven years of travel, he has explored hundreds of cities, towns, and villages around the world and has met countless people from all walks of life. Worldschooling created the opportunity to connect with people of all ages, economic and social backgrounds, belief systems, nationalities, and professions. A key component of worldschooling is valuing conversations with diverse people and different worldviews. We gain a broader understanding of the world around us through conversation.

Learn to Recognize Worldviews—Through exposure to new ideas, concepts and cultural practices, worldschoolers are given the opportunity to learn about beliefs that differ from their own and to confront any internal biases they might hold. By looking at the world from another perspective, we are able to achieve a higher level of respect and understanding, and this is something that we seek to do through travel. Worldschooling experiences are impactful and capable of shifting the way we look at the world and the people in it, and this is just one way that we can make the world a more peaceful planet.

Language Learning Through Immersion and Play—Researchers claim that the young minds have more dynamic structures enabling them to learn languages more rapidly than adults do. In our travels, I observed ten-year-old Miro immerse himself into language learning without effort or fear and learn naturally just as he learned his native language. Through play, he interacted with local children and through his own desire to understand, he was able to absorb vocabulary and syntax effortlessly. As a result, eleven years later, Miro is a fluent Spanish speaker without ever attending a Spanish class.

Receive a Worldly Education in Context—Contrary to traditional education which generally places the subject outside of oneself without context or involvement to one's own life, learning in a worldschooling environment creates an active relationship to that which we are learning. In other words, it's impossible not to learn (at least a little without effort) about the Incas as we tour Machu Picchu, because it is our body walking through the ruins, having the experience that includes active learning, taking in the sights and sounds. Where we go from there is up to the individual learner and the layering of that information adds value to our experiences. These experiences become relevant in our memories and build a deeper relationship to the lessons we are learning.

Lainie Liberti is a radically unschooling mom, author, speaker, community leader, teen coach, and alternative education advocate who helped to spearhead the thriving worldschooling movement. Liberti has spoken about worldschooling on the TEDx Edu stage in Amsterdam, written about learning through travel for multiple magazines, academic journals, and web sites including *International Journal of Education, Journal of Unschooling and Alternative Learning, People Magazine, Huffington Post, USA Today, The New York Times,* and *The New York Post* and has contributed to several books on the topic of worldschooling.

Lainie co-foundered Project World School with her son in 2012. Liberty designs and co-facilitates the Project World School teen retreats as month-long immersive learning communities to support self-directed teens from around the world. Over the last 8 years, Lainie has facilitated 20+ international retreats for almost 100 teens, learning through cultural immersion, examining personal values, and exploring world views. Lainie is also the founder and creator of Transformative Mentoring for Teens that launched in early 2020 offering virtual 1:1 coaching for teens as well as a 12-week course designed to transform lives. Lainie is a certified life coach, specializing in transformational coaching. Her new book, *Seen, Heard, and Understood: Parenting and Partnering with Teens for Greater Mental Health* came out in August of 2022.

Ken Danford

Expanding the Movement: Attracting More People to Self-Directed Learning

Ken Danford

In January 2020, I wrote a blog titled, "Where is Everybody?" Having just completed our 26th year of offering a quality program and with alumni approaching and passing 40 years old, North Star continues to attract 50-70 teens per year. In a community of perhaps 5000 students in grades 7-12, I feel our student population is missing a "0," off by a magnitude of hundreds. This is not a North Star problem: one could go around the United States and count up all the teens in democratic free schools, Agile Learning Centers, Liberated Learners centers, and other self-directed learning programs, and be hard-pressed to match the population of one large public high school. One could then count up all the independent unschooling teens over age 15 and maybe have enough students to match a second large public high school. For all of our ability to improve people's lives, the mainstream is still not joining our party. Why?

In the self-directed learning community, out here at the end of the schooling spectrum rainbow, we are doing a lot of things right. We are creating programs that really work—in terms of learning, in terms of social and emotional growth, and in terms of successful outcomes. Many of us are doing so in ways that are affordable and inclusive. We empower students and families to design their own learning, we take "no" for an answer to our well-intentioned and impressive array of offerings and invitations, and we see our alumni succeed as college students, workers, and entrepreneurs.

While we have some important differences among our programs, one thing we have in common is that we all want to be serving more children and teens in our communities. One other similarity we possess is that our collective set of schools and programs appeal mainly to white people. In this era of COVID-19 and Black Lives Matter, I am more conscious than ever of this limitation. However, even among white people, we aren't all that popular, either. After a solid 50 years or more of results that prove we know what we are doing in this field of self-directed learning, I am interested in considering whether 2022 offers us any fresh ideas to consider.

North Star receives at least one hundred inquiries per year from parents interested in learning about our program. I have handled most of these conversations personally over the years, as it is something I particularly enjoy doing. I have had at least two-thousand initial conversations, and I still find them a favorite part of my week. Perhaps half of these conversations proceed to in-person meetings, and perhaps half of those meetings result in new members for North Star. For the sake of this book chapter, I want to reflect on those families that don't join North Star, and even more, on those people who don't even call us to learn about our program. (If you want to learn about those families that do choose to join North Star, please read my book!)

The Speech That Doesn't Work:

Ken Danford

In this book chapter, I use the terms "homeschooling" and "unschooling" and "self-directed learning" interchangeably, acknowledging that "homeschooling" is the legal term for the activity and that families fall along a spectrum of how they choose to homeschool.

In my first conversations with inquiring parents, I often make three assertions that support our slogan, "School is optional." I say:

1. School is optional for learning.
2. School is optional for credentialing.
3. School is optional, in a positive sense. I believe school is a fine option for people who wish to attend and choose it as the way they wish to live their lives.

Let me review where we lose people:

1. School is optional for learning.

Parents and teens will acknowledge that some other kids may learn math and science and foreign language on their own, or read books for the sheer fun of it, without school assignments and grades. But they imagine that anyone who does such things is uniquely motivated and mature (or nerdy), and that nobody in their family would ever behave that way. Inquiring parents will also accept the premise that some other people's kids actually pursue art, or music, or outdoor activities in a serious way, but they are certain their child will not. Teens will believe that other kids have started businesses, become social activists, or found interesting ways to volunteer in the community, but they don't see themselves doing so.

In other words, teens and parents can be persuaded that other people can and do learn without school, but many simply don't trust themselves with this sort of freedom. They feel fairly certain that they will just play video games, eat snacks, and sleep. My job shifts from persuading them that they "can" learn without school requirements to the concept that "they" can learn without school requirements. These are people I don't really know, and in the first few minutes after meeting them I'm giving them a pep talk about their innate capacity to set goals, develop plans, and follow through. It's a bit audacious, I suppose.

Nevertheless, the key point here is that while I insist on winning the intellectual argument that people are learning all sorts of things without school demands, I often encounter resistance that this idea applies to the people with whom I'm speaking. And so ends these conversations.

2. School is optional for credentialing.

Uh-oh. Now we're getting on to some seriously shaky ground. Say what? North Star doesn't give diplomas? Click goes the phone. In meetings, parents and teens are preparing to get up and leave.

"Wait!" I say. "Hang on for a moment, and listen to this next part. Then we can stop if you want."

I explain that for fifty years, homeschoolers and others who have homeschooled independently or attended un-accredited private schools have successfully moved on to college, including places such as all five local colleges including Amherst College (my alma mater and locally elite institution), Hampshire College (local alternative college,) the University of Massachusetts (by the hundreds, including at the UMass Honors College,) and Smith College and Mt. Holyoke College (also elite, private liberal arts colleges). These are in addition to all of the colleges and programs across the country which North Star alumni have attended since around the year 2000.

I identify and explain some alternative credentials that independent learners receive if they are not in a private school: the General Education Diploma (GED) credential (most commonly used by North Star families and how it is not second-class, but rather a 100% useful credential); Self-Certification (some homeschoolers make their own diplomas and how a certain small subset of North Star families find this appealing); Online Accreditation (online homeschool programs that offer accredited diplomas, and how that is occasionally used by North Star families). I further mention that some teens manage quite well with no accreditation at all, but I don't push that topic with new, skeptical families. I want to note here that my comments are specific to Massachusetts. In other states, there are ways for homeschoolers to receive a high school diploma or other official accreditation from the public school system.

As people familiar with the homeschooling movement know quite well, homeschoolers have had tremendous success moving on to four-year colleges.

They often begin by taking classes at community colleges as part of their high school-homeschooling experience, and then take those credits with them when they transfer. It turns out that a student who opts out of school, gets a GED or other accreditation, and starts with community college might save two years-worth of four-year college expenses and time! In fact, this fear of "losing years" is backwards, I claim in a flourish! The response is often underwhelming eye-rolling. "My kid is not getting a GED. We insist on a regular high school diploma for everyone in our family."

I continue to assert that if college isn't the likely next step, a homeschooling approach offers teens a major head-start on trying out part-time jobs, exploring interests, or starting their own businesses. Teens begin to shift uncomfortably, confronted with the opportunity to skip bumbling through high school for several more years and to get on with life right now. This new option seems harder, scarier, and much more trouble than simply laying low and being a mildly irresponsible teen until high school graduation. And so ends these meetings.

3. School is optional, in a positive sense!

Then I cheerfully shift to the third point: School is optional! As in, you might really choose it! I would have stuck with the known path of schooling, had anyone offered me the choice to opt out back in the 1980s. My children both chose to attend school. Many North Star teens have siblings that choose to attend school. In fact, many North Star teens use our program for middle school only and then opt back into high school. I suddenly shift gears and tell these inquirers to North Star that school can work perfectly well for many people, and they are welcome to choose it. I just want them to understand their options and make a conscious choice.

"Great!" say teens, who often prefer to stay with their friends in school and the regular program no matter how dismal their day-to-day experience may have become for them. And so off they go, re-committing themselves to making school work this time.

COVID-19 Pandemic Observations

As I watched families struggle during the early part of the pandemic, I feel reminded of how much people count on school. Parents rely on school as a place to send their children during the day. They hope that perhaps their children will learn some new and interesting things there that they are not learning at home. They also hope their children will meet some new people and make some friends. Maybe their children will join a sport or find a hobby through school. Teens rely on school as a place to go, away from their homes and parents, to make friends and meet some encouraging and helpful adults. With any luck, they will "learn what they need to know" to succeed in life.

As parents, educators, civic leaders, and sometimes even students commented on "online-school-at-home" when many schools were closed during 2020-2021, I heard the desire for things to "get back to normal." Which to me, mostly meant having a safe place where children can go during the day, regardless of how much they learn while there. The media consensus that I witnessed treated "kids out of school" as "fish out of water." The dominant assumption was that kids who were not attending school in-person were not learning and were falling behind.

I suggest that instead we use a different analogy, such as "schools closed" are like "restaurants closed." The loss of the "sitting in restaurants" means that "people have to do more cooking at home," offering not only responsibility but also opportunity. "Cooking at home" could be seen as a boring chore, but it could also be a chance for fun learning and bold experiments. In fact, the need for more "cooking at home" might lead to skill-development that inspires life-changing confidence for some young people.

In addition, what I saw in the mainstream rush to what people were calling "homeschooling" during the pandemic reflects an assumption of parents teaching their children the "core curriculum" with mostly familiar techniques. We were not seeing much about self-directed learning that proposes young people might learn any variety of content in any number of ways. Our message was not a significant part of the conversation I was hearing when it came to "Pandemic Pods" or public school-hybrid models of attendance during this crisis.

Two Major Obstacles: Money and Transportation

In the past, I have written and stated in many places that I think the major obstacles to having more people join North Star and other self-directed learning programs have been money and transportation. Public schools are free, and they have yellow buses that go around the community to give people rides. I have seen the overwhelming importance of these logistical issues. In my meetings with prospective families, I have concluded that concerns about the practical topics of money and rides often far outweigh the philosophical considerations outlined above. I imagine this is true for most private alternative schools and programs, especially those featuring self-directed learning.

North Star has done a lot to deal with both of these issues. In terms of tuition, our fees are modest ($9,500 - $3,650 sliding scale per year) and we offer fee reductions to any family that needs to pay less than the low end of the sliding scale. We have welcomed every interested family for 26 years. We are not alone. Many programs offer tuition that is far less than conventional private schools, and make efforts to include low-income families. Nevertheless, most families in our community in western Massachusetts don't have $5,000 or more per year per child to spend on school, especially when the alternative is free (public school/charter school/vocational school.)

North Star has been in four locations, always centrally located on a public bus route. We help our members to arrange carpools, and our staff have always been willing to drive teens who live in their neighborhoods. We do the best we can to minimize the difficulties of transportation. Of course, it is not always enough.

Money and transportation are serious issues. But in most cases, they are manageable for people who

investigate North Star and want to join our program. I
want to think more about the people who cut off our
conversations or don't even inquire in the first
place. These thoughts bring me back to the issues of
families that demand "Learning by Assignments" and
"Diplomas" and dismiss self-directed learning options.

A Two-Part Thought Experiment

To think through these issues, I would like to
name two sets of families that have not found North Star
particularly appealing, and then offer a proposal for each
group that holds firm to the principles of self-directed
learning but that offer a vision that feels more
usable. The groups are BIPOC families (Black,
Indigenous, and People of Color) and families using
conventional private schools.

Group One: BIPOC Families

When I left my teaching job in the Amherst
Regional Public Schools, I had hoped that some BIPOC
students would join our program. While that did happen
with a few individual students, the trickle never
developed into a stream. This book chapter is not the
place to revisit this topic fully, though the wish for more
diversity does feel fresh and important in 2022 given the
rise of Black Lives Matter and renewed concerns for race
relations in our community. Briefly, I understand the
limits and my personal responsibility for the reality that
North Star was founded by two white men (Joshua
Hornick and myself), and that over the years almost all

of our staff and Board members have been white people. For context, North Star is located in a predominantly white community in Hampshire and Franklin Counties of western Massachusetts, where less than 20% of students and families would identify as BIPOC.

I know that around the country, the number of BIPOC families choosing homeschooling is increasing quite rapidly, with positive results. There are many reasons that BIPOC families might seek an alternative to public school, and I have met several speakers, writers, and educators deeply involved in spreading the self-directed learning approach specifically to these families. In 2021, I co-facilitated a course called Another Way with Lora Smothers, who is now creating the Joy Village School in Athens, GA, a school that is "centering the joy and thriving of Black youth." The other facilitators of Another Way, Sundiata Soon-Jahta and Cassidy Younghans, share these priorities as well.

However, I believe that for many BIPOC parents, the idea of opting out of regular schooling in favor of "schooling-at-home" already stretches their boundaries, and the prospect of self-directed learning is a bridge too far. In a very traditional and concerned sort of way, these parents expect schools to teach their kids what they need to know. They are not convinced that "learning what one wants, when one wants, as much as one wants" will get their children very far in the harsh conventional world built on systemic racism. They want their children to play by the rules, master the game, and move on with unimpeachable credentials. They are not interested in the risks of having their children grow up outside the system and facing the consequences later. I hear echoes of my Jewish grandparents and other white immigrants from a century ago in these concerns. There is not much space to negotiate when BIPOC parents state: "My children need to go to a school that will make them learn essential things, hold them accountable, and certify their outcomes." Again, I hear these reservations frequently from white parents as well who dismiss North Star, but with less consistency.

Further, for much of the past century, BIPOC families have been fighting for access to good public schools. Opting out of public or private conventional schooling is abandoning a dominant civil rights battle of one's parents and grandparents. It is not easily done. For this proposal, I am going to bypass the local BIPOC teens in western MA and also the BIPOC students in my suburban hometown of Shaker Heights, Ohio. (Shaker Heights High School and a program I helped start in 1983, the Student Group on Race Relations, were featured in August 2020 on CNN's United Shades of America with W. Kamau Bell.) I will aim this proposal at a more urban, predominantly BIPOC community where I had my first teaching job in the 1990s at Andrew Jackson Middle School in Suitland, Maryland (Prince George's County just outside of Washington, D.C.):

- Take two housing units in a public housing complex and convert them into a unified learning center of perhaps 3000-5000 square feet.
- Fund three positions for staff members from the local community

who would be known and trusted to the children and families living there.

- Have these staff members recruit up to 30 children who want an alternative to their public school option, and support them to fill out homeschooling paperwork.
- Host a learning program right where the kids live—no transportation issues for children, much less difficulty connecting with parents and guardians.
- Run a thoughtful learning center, much like a high-quality afterschool or summer program.
- Do so with a commitment to unschooling and self-directed learning rather than implementing a prescribed online or conventional school curriculum.
- Encourage the students to spend time at the learning center, and also out in the community for additional classes, volunteer work, paid jobs, and other activities.
- Connect the high-school-age students with local community colleges for enrollment in early-college programs and local private or state universities where they might audit courses.
- Support each teen to develop a portfolio or personal transcript that

> documents and describes their activities.
> - Encourage each teen to get a GED or other available credential in their state when they feel ready to move on to the next phase of their lives.
> - Introduce families to young adult alumni of self-directed learning who can share their paths and help teens create their own visions for the future.
> - Support the families and the larger community to understand how learning in this way will work out at least as well, and in some cases better than, remaining at the local public high school through graduation.
> - Fully fund this program so that it has limited costs (i.e., incidental supplies) to its participating families.

My guess is that such a program would "work," in the sense that its "graduates" would be at least as well off as if they had remained in public school. My white privilege perhaps allows me to speculate that BIPOC teens who would get a head start on life in this way, amass some community college credits, and move on to young adulthood with a strong sense of self-awareness and a healthy range of experiences would be able to confront and overcome the systemic racism they would encounter at least as effectively as their peers who remained in school for the duration. I would like to support a serious attempt to see what would be involved

Ken Danford

in making this approach more possible for BIPOC students, especially those living where few self-directed learning programs exist.

Still, this idea would hinge on finding some families who would trust the program enough to allow their children to pursue self-directed learning and aim for a GED or other available credential instead of a public high school diploma. I see that this proposal does not address the concerns I have listed above, but I don't see a way to combine "making sure" students learn things and "conferring diplomas" with the essential freedom of self-directed learning. For those of you wanting to explore such a compromise, a terrific model to investigate is LighthouseHolyoke, founded by former North Star Program Director Catherine Gobron in Holyoke, MA. Lighthouse is now an officially accredited private school.

Group Two: Families using Conventional Private Schools

A second group of families we rarely see at North Star, and more broadly in the field of self-directed learning, is families who have chosen to use conventional private schools, including BIPOC families, with the goal of seeing their children gain acceptance to competitive private colleges. I live near Deerfield Academy, Northfield-Mt. Hermon, and several other rigorous private "prep schools," in addition to a solid number of religious-based private schools. (I am more or less excluding alternative approaches such as Montessori, Waldorf, and progressive private schools

134

from this commentary about conventional "prep" schools.) Some of these schools prioritize race and class diversity, and make an effort to be inclusive, and these efforts may be expanding in 2022.

I think about the families who choose these conventional options and wonder whether there is any way to make our approach more appealing. We know that some of the children who attend these schools are miserable. These schools often pride themselves on how "rigorous" their curricula are, and many students find the academic and social pressure to be either unpleasant or downright unbearable. Families choosing to pay the tuition at these schools could afford to join a self-directed learning program and also hire tutors, fund hobbies, or pay for special adventures. The traditional private school approach is not particularly "progressive" or "alternative" compared to public schools. The high tuitions and huge time demands (long days, required sports, and more) seem wildly inefficient to me for children who aren't thriving in those settings, and I feel sad for the kids suffering a bad fit. Further, we know that homeschooling teens often end up in the same colleges as these private prep school students, frequently with a year or two of college credits under their belts! We know there is a different means to a similar end for those committed to four-year college experiences.

Ironically, the concerns and objections of these private school parents to North Star sound quite similar to those of the first group of disbelievers: "My child needs to be in a challenging environment with demanding teachers in order to learn." "We don't trust that your outcome will be respected or valued by the wider culture we want our children to enter after high school." "What you do is fine for those other kids, but it's not for our family."

For this proposal, I'd like to lift the model I wrote above for families in a low-income housing complex and move it to the bucolic setting of Amherst College. Those Amherst folks might find 3000-5000 square feet they can spare? They could hire a few staff to help advise, teach, and manage 30 or more students who choose legal homeschooling instead of regular schooling. They could connect them to local community programs and opportunities, and as they grow older, help them meet Amherst College students and professors and encourage them to audit classes on campus. Again, I would insist on an unschooling approach with no coercion.

Imagine these students "graduate" from an alternative learning program at Amherst College, and have letters of recommendation from Amherst College staff? In the history of alternative education, there were experiments and trends in this direction in the 1960s and 1970s, but the concept sounds completely radical at this time. I will confidently assert here that "Of course it would work!" Amherst College, I'm waiting for a call.

Summary

I think it may be fair to conclude that what most parents are looking for from schooling is an interesting and enjoyable experience that will put their children on a solid road to college admissions and future success. While many families may be willing to concede that self-directed learning may have potential for being more interesting and enjoyable than conventional school, they are doubtful that it will be a better method for long-term success. BIPOC families distrust the notion that their children will get the same social welcoming that white children may receive after growing up without schooling; conventional private school families doubt the idea that growing up in freedom will carry more benefits than the social capital gained from going through elite private schools. I venture to guess that the majority of mainstream parents share these concerns about the touted outcomes of self-directed learning programs. These parents may all be correct to some extent (especially regarding whether self-directed learning is a good match for their particular families,) though I will continue to find people willing to take these risks and then report out the results to the world. I remain deeply optimistic about our culture's openness to children who choose to learn outside of conventional schooling.

Imagine a culture where programs challenging the need for coerced learning and standard high school diplomas are easily accessible, widely available, and institutionally respected. These programs could be offered in ways that address the concerns of students and parents, both philosophically and logistically. It's not that hard to imagine this world; one could start by reflecting on the impressive range of exciting afterschool programs and summer camps that feel familiar and valuable.

Conceptually, we know that all kinds of learning, including academic learning, can happen in this way.

Ken Danford

Let's celebrate and embrace the moments, the resources, the people, and the systems that promote learning. Let's not worry if the learning "counts" towards certification. Let's believe that children who spend time becoming experts at one thing might use that experience to become good at something else, or even to address their weaknesses when they feel the need has arrived. Let's develop the faith and confidence that children who learn in this way will in fact be able to gain admission to colleges, obtain interesting jobs, and mature into competent young adults.

In twenty-six years of working in self-directed learning, I have witnessed the demographics of homeschoolers enlarge to most of the culture. Back in the 1980s and early 1990s, the stereotype was that homeschooling was for religious people (mostly conservative Christians) or for white people engaged in various counter-cultural lifestyles. It wasn't really true, ever, but over the past decades the families utilizing homeschooling have grown into the millions, involving at least 3% of school-age children. The reasons for homeschooling have expanded into quite simple and pedestrian statements: "My child was having a bad year," or, "We just wanted to try something different." Homeschooling is not a lifelong commitment, and many families use it as a short-term alternative. Especially at North Star, we see families in which one or more children are homeschooling while others choose to attend school. The world can be fluid, accommodating, and simple.

As of the summer of 2022, we are still in the midst of the pandemic. North Star received a surge of inquiries this past winter and spring, and I've speculated that perhaps the increase is pandemic-related. I wonder if young people are resisting going back to "full-time school" just as many adults are resisting going back to "full-time office work." I also believe the pandemic has destigmatized homeschooling somewhat, and has made our approach of having a day-time community center to make homeschooling more available and sustainable far more interesting.

In addition to the pandemic, we all have a lot to cope with in our lives. If schooling is helping our families understand and respond to these challenges, then by all means we should continue sending our children and supporting these institutions. If, on the other hand, schooling is adding one more stressful element to our lives, we need to share what we know about alternatives and make these options ever more accessible and appealing to our neighbors.

Kenneth Danford is the Co-Founder and Executive Director of North Star: Self-Directed Learning for Teens. Founded in 1996, North Star's mission is to support teens who feel constrained by schooling to embark on homeschooling. North Star is a community center in Sunderland, MA, that offers classes, tutorials, social opportunities, and many more activities for its members. North Star members have a weekly private meeting with an advisor to discuss how they feel about their learning experiences. Advisors meet regularly with parents and teens together to review goals and assess progress.

Ken Danford

North Star members move on successfully to college, work, and young adulthood, often many steps ahead of their school-based peers in both achievement and self-awareness. Kenneth shares a much fuller version of the North Star story in his 2019 book: *Learning is Natural, School is Optional: The North Star Approach to Offering Teens a Head Start on Life.*

Kenneth has been an enthusiastic presenter and attendee at the Alternative Education Resource Organization's annual conference since 2007, served as a "Superhost" at the 2020 Homeschooling Global Summit, and is an active participant with the Alliance for Self-Directed Education. Kenneth provides consulting and support to spread the North Star approach through the Liberated Learners network, which now consists of about a dozen centers around the United States, Canada, and in Manila, The Philippines.

See:

www.northstarteens.org
www.liberatedlearners.net
www.kennethdanford.com

Chapter 8

Alpha II Alternative School

Carol Nash

Introduction

Alpha II Alternative School is a grades 7-12 public school with the Toronto District School Board founded over the 2006/7 academic year by nine parents of ALPHA Alternative School—Toronto's oldest public alternative elementary school. Alpha II is now in its fifteenth year as a real choice for families who support unschooling. For those families who have come from a homeschooling background, Alpha II is often the first school these families have attended. It is possibly the only school world-wide that has continuously maintained unschooling principles in a fully publicly supported setting.

There are no grades, no marks, no standardized evaluations, and no report cards at Alpha II. The students (referred to as mentees) keep a record of the work they consider valuable in personal portfolios. At least twice a year, families meet with the teachers (called mentors) to discuss how it is that together—and in relation to the other mentees—they can facilitate the learning the mentee considers important. Post-secondary school is one, though not the only, option mentees may want to pursue after Alpha II. Those who are interested in post-secondary learning may apply directly from Alpha II by gearing their personal portfolios to the requirements of the programs they desire to attend. As such, they apply to post-secondary programs as homeschoolers might.

141

Carol Nash

The number of mentees enrolled in Alpha II has ranged from 17 in the first year of the school to 90 in the school's fifth year. During the 2021/22 school year, there were 20 mentees with two full-time and one part-time mentor. The mentors and the principal are selected from among those Toronto District School board teachers and principals who meet the criteria determined by the Alpha II community, reestablished on a yearly basis in the School Statement of Needs.

Alpha II, currently is housed along with Bloor Collegiate Institute in Central Technical School while the new building for both Alpha II and Bloor is being constructed beside the previous site that served both schools. This area where the new school is under construction is part of what was a larger campus of schools chosen by the co-founders in 2007 as the most suitable location in the city for the school because of its proximity to the subway, a large park, a shopping mall and a vibrant community. The site, purchased for redevelopment as condominiums, includes a new building for both schools at the westerly end of the site.

The school serves those interested in unschooling principles from anywhere in Ontario (the province in which Toronto is located) who have the ability to get to the school on a regular basis. Although the majority of the mentees are from the Toronto area, a significant number come from cities and towns outside the city, some of them over one and a half hours away. With few unschooling options available in North America, and even fewer in public schools, previous families have moved from as far away as California to enroll in Alpha II.

ALPHA is an acronym for A Lot of People Hoping for an Alternative. The original elementary school was founded in 1972 in response to a document put out by the Ontario government in 1968 called *Living and Learning* based on Article 26 of the Declaration of Human Rights.

Article 26

1. Everyone has the right to education. Education shall be free, at least in the elementary and fundamental stages. Elementary education shall be compulsory. Technical and professional education shall be made generally available and higher education shall be equally accessible to all on the basis of merit.
2. Education shall be directed to the full development of the human personality and to the strengthening of respect for human rights and fundamental freedoms. It shall promote understanding, tolerance and friendship among all nations, racial or religious groups, and shall further the activities of the United Nations for the maintenance of peace.
3. Parents have a prior right to choose the kind of education that shall be given to their children.

Also influential in the founding of the original ALPHA elementary was the educational philosophy presented in the North American edition of the book

Summerhill by A.S. Neil (an important reference in creating *Living and Learning*). Other important references included *Deschooling Society* by Ivan Illich, *Pedagogy of the Oppressed* by Latin American educator Paulo Freire, and the work of teacher John Holt as the originator of the term "unschooling," especially his 1964 book, *How Children Fail*.

In that Article 26 stipulates elementary education shall be compulsory, the founders of Alpha II pointed out during the school's creation that unschoolers had the right to have their philosophy of education a choice in the public system as compulsory education in any other form was contrary to the beliefs of unschooling parents. As such, to not provide the option for unschooling in the public system would be contrary to point 3 of Article 26. Furthermore, the value of the unschooling philosophy is that it is fully in support of point 2 of Article 26.

When concentrated work on founding Alpha II began in 2006, ALPHA—an elementary school that initially went to grade 8—was a junior kindergarten to grade 6 school with no physical room for expansion. This meant at that time no unschooling option was available for the elementary grades 7 and 8 and the compulsory education students could choose from after leaving ALPHA no longer included unschooling in the public board.

Given this lack of a continuing unschool option beyond grade 6, there is no obvious reason why it took 34 years of ALPHAs existence for parents to work together to form Alpha II. Nevertheless, there may have been no other time more suitable for its creation. Five of the nine parents involved had doctorates in their respective fields and had been involved with program formation in other educational institutions. Moreover, the principal of ALPHA was supportive, as were the school trustees, superintendents and Board itself. Given that *Living and Learning,* which was intended to be a blueprint for all education in Ontario leading to the year 2000, was set aside after only seven years, it may be that those Board officials in 2007 when Alpha II was approved were wanting to reaffirm Toronto as an innovator in alternative education. As such, these officials saw the benefit to reestablishing the tenets of self-directed learning laid out in *Living and Learning* in a grades 7-12 model.

What is Alpha II?

Alpha II is a public school where people self-direct in response to a passion for learning with respect to what they personally value. At the same time, they must be willing and able to be part of a community based on consensus where each person's voice counts in developing that consensus. To understand Alpha II and how it operates, it is important to realize the meaning of the essential words in this description of Alpha II. An explanation of each follows in the order these fundamental words appear in the above description of the school.

Public School

Carol Nash

Alpha II is supported entirely by Ontario taxpayers. The resources it gets are determined by a formula in relation to the number of young people enrolled. Included in the resources available to Alpha II are the space for the school, the mentors hired, equipment, supplies, caretaking and administration. Since the school is from grades 7-12, this means there are two teacher unions from which the mentors are hired. The elementary union provides the mentors for grades 7-8 and the secondary union for the grades 9-12. The Alpha II community develops criteria for the hiring of mentors, but the principal is responsible for hiring and must supervise the mentors based on the contracts negotiated between the teacher unions and the Toronto District School Board. Every effort is made to ensure the teachers hired as mentors at Alpha II understand and support unschooling principals and are self-directed learners themselves.

People

The people involved with Alpha II include the following: the mentees (the young people enrolled in grades 7-12), the mentors (elementary and secondary teachers), parents/guardians, administrators (principal, vice-principal, assistant), the school trustee, the school superintendent, and the volunteers who help to bring additional offerings to the school.

Self-Direct

Those associated with Alpha II believe they can affect their life because they consider they have a point of view worth holding, developing, supporting, recording as part of their personal portfolios and sharing. Furthermore, they understand it is up to them to take responsibility for the outcome of their actions. These are the things that define self-direction at Alpha II. This differs from self-expression, where people do what they want, when they want, how they want. Alpha II is a place designed for self-direction in contrast to self-expression.

Passion for Learning

To have a passion for learning, as it is defined at Alpha II, people must have a motivation that inspires them and continues their interest. This motivation encourages them to seek out resources and mentors in finding a time and space for their passion to be expressed. As self-directed learners, mentees determine the optimal results and what they consider worth recording in their personal portfolios regarding their passion for learning.

Personally Value

No person at Alpha II is asked to engage in activities they do not personally value. To personally value something means to be guided by a personally meaningful approach to life. This encourages learning that is inspired, purposeful and something with which the person can be proud. When people personally value what they do, they demonstrate this by wanting to continue to improve their work then record it effectively in their personal portfolios and share the results in whatever way they define as meaningful.

Willing and Able

People participate at Alpha II because they are interested in being involved in self-directing their learning as part of a community rather than entirely on their own. Furthermore, they are able to identify different points of view by, 1) communicating their own effectively, and 2) getting to know those of others through first wanting to understand and then creating a time and space to do so. What's most important is listening carefully and non-judgmentally while considering differences.

Community

The people associated with Alpha II are community members. They demonstrate their membership by self-directing their activities and caring about the shared resources. Sharing those resources involves finding a time and place for anyone who wants to use them to do so and maintaining them in a condition where they can be used when wanted. In order to be effective members, each person needs to focus on knowing their own point of view and looking to understand the points of view of others. The aim is to concentrate on finding ways to include all members.

Chapter 8

Consensus

Consensus at Alpha II differs from each of agreement, compromise and giving in. Instead, it represents various points of view as equal through adding together all voices and finding a time and a place to do what each member personally values. This is done by considering how each voice in the Alpha II community affects others and by seeking ways to encourage what it is each member personally values.

Founding Pillars of Alpha II

As all members of the school come to know regularly at meetings and in other forms of communication, Alpha II is founded on two pillars: 1) self-directed learning, and 2) a community based on consensus decision making in which each person's voice counts equally in developing the consensus.

In identifying young people who are a good fit for the school as self-directed learners, an extensive admissions procedure has been developed over the years. Those who are admitted have toured the school with their families, filled out an application form outlining their interests and provided examples of their self-directed learning. As well, each applicant comes for a trial visit at the school of approximately a week. If the applicant is admitted, a meeting with the family is held to determine if the mentee feels that their time at Alpha II will be effective based on what the mentee values. If the school and the family don't feel that Alpha II is a good fit this represents a time when an exit is appropriate; otherwise, the mentee is invited to begin.

What Self-Direction Looks Like at Alpha II

What self-direction looks like at Alpha II is varied. There is a large main classroom that includes a hang-out area, computers, and an attached music room. As well, there is both a separate art room and multi-purpose room. However, what happens in the school is only part of what represents Alpha II. Mentees can also find mentors in their areas of interest outside the school. Examples are assisting an ornithologist at the Royal Ontario Museum, working at a car body shop, and participating in the dual credits program at a number of the community colleges in Toronto. For those thinking of going on to post-secondary education after they leave Alpha II, the dual credits program gives them credits at the post-secondary level and helps to increase the suitability of their portfolio in this regard.

Unlike many other democratic schools based on the idea of young people's votes deciding the direction of the school, there is no voting at Alpha II. The reason is that, in a school that sees its foundation as self-directed learning, if one's ideas are voted down at a meeting then this means that group decision making has become more important than self-direction. To ensure that self-direction is not abandoned in group decision making, a time and a place are found to do what each person desires. As such, the decision is not to find one solution, it is to find a way to accommodate what everyone values.

How the school is able to take each person's point of view into consideration is through the weekly meeting. This meeting is where the idea of consensus decision making for school-wide matters is most evident. The purpose of the meeting is to determine how resources will be shared among mentees through finding a time and place where they can be made available when and where they are required.

To determine what are the needs of mentees, the meeting takes place in a circle permitting mentees the opportunity to give their point of view one at a time regarding issues on the meeting's agenda. Using this circle format, each person expresses their preference regarding the particular issue being discussed on the agenda. Once these preferences are known, rather than debating what is the best response, each point of view is considered equally and a time and place is found to do what each person prefers. In this way, the importance of self-direction is maintained through the decision-making process.

Core Values

As a Toronto District School Board alternative school, every 5 years Alpha II is asked to reconsider its core values that differentiate the school from all other Toronto alternative schools. In the most recent core values document submitted to the Board January 2020, the Alpha II community indicated how the two core pillars of self-direction and community based on consensus are broken down and put into practice. Unlike some other Toronto alternative schools that have seen

Carol Nash

major changes to their core values over the years, Alpha
IIs core values are essentially the same as those the
founding parents created when the school was approved
by the Board in 2007. The focus of Alpha IIs core values
is first stating the value and then indicating a practice
that represents the value. In refining these core values
every five years, it is important to be very specific in
identifying how the school differs from other alternative
schools to continue support from the Board. These core
values are then posted on the school's website.

Core Values of the Alpha II Community Self-Direction:

Learning is meaningful

Value: Students (mentees) learn best when what they are
learning is meaningful to them and they have been
centrally involved in deciding what and how to learn.
Practice: Students (mentees), in communication with
teachers (mentors) determine what and how they would
like to learn.

Freedom Provided

Value: Alpha II provides freedom to choose by
providing a rich range of learning opportunities for
students (mentees) to engage them and enthusiastically
supports students (mentees) in designing their own
learning activities.
Practice: Students (mentees), in consultation with
teachers (mentors), are encouraged to actively seek out

152

materials, equipment, information, and learning experiences to support their learning plans and goals as well as to expand their horizons.

Responsibility Supported

Value: Students (mentees) are enthusiastically supported to be responsible for their learning within an atmosphere of non-coercion.
Practice: Teachers are mentors rather than directors. They support students (mentees) by encouraging them to take responsibility for pursuing a wide and deep exploration of their interests.

No Standardized Expectations

Value: Students (mentees) learn in unique ways; no predetermined or standardized expectations are placed on students (mentees).
Practice: Students (mentees) record their own learning when and how they deem appropriate in personal portfolios.

No Predetermined Schedules

Value: When and where the student (mentee) learns is determined by the student (mentee) based on their interests and resources available, not by a predetermined, standardized schedule.
Practice: Flexible attendance of students (mentees) participating in off-site learning and personal programs (such as Co-Op and Dual Credit, community support,

Carol Nash

and community involvement) means that consistent communication between parents and mentors is essential to maintain student (mentee) safety.

Comments and Observations

Value: Teachers (mentors) provide students (mentees) with Comments and Observations rather than evaluations.
Practice: Comments and Observations are provided by teachers (mentors) and students (mentees) on an ongoing basis and when formally requested. They also can be provided at student (mentee)—parent/guardian—teacher (mentor) conferences where interests and personal goals are discussed. Notes taken at the conference are for the student (mentee) to add to their portfolio if they so choose. Grades, tests and report cards are not part of the Alpha II school culture or philosophy.

Community Based on Consensus:

Inclusive of All

Value: Alpha II strives to create a positive environment inclusive of all.
Practice: Everyone at Alpha II is encouraged to listen carefully to others' points of view and, when making shared school-related decisions, find a time and place to do what each person values.

Voices Added Together

Value: The school is run as a Community based on consensus where consensus mean each person's voice is added together in developing that consensus. Voting and majority rule are not featured. The aim of decision making and conflict resolution is finding win/win solutions for shared resources.

Practice: Significant decisions about the school are decided by a consensus method permitting everyone to be heard on each issue at monthly Community Meetings. These meetings are attended by administrators, teachers (mentors), students (mentees) and parents/guardians. Local classroom decisions are made by a consensus of all points of view at weekly student (mentee)-teacher (mentor) meetings.

Respect for Abilities

Value: Respecting each person's ability to self-direct their learning and adding their point of view to the consensus are necessary in fostering a learning environment that permits students (mentees) to feel safe and encouraged to learn.

Practice: Everyone involved in Alpha II (students (mentees), administrators, teachers (mentors), parents/guardians, volunteers) is encouraged to listen carefully, attentively and supportively to what others say. Disagreements are resolved through a conflict resolution process including teachers (mentors) but initiated by students (mentees). This process engages each person involved in the conflict to provide their point of view and then, together, finding a time and place for all proposed outcomes to be realized.

Conclusion

Alpha II Alternative School is unique in the world as it is an alternative school that has been fully publicly supported during its entire history and continually has maintained its founding core values of self-direction in a community based on consensus.

Although the mentees who attend Alpha II do not formally graduate, many have gone on to not only work in their area of interest and expertise, some have also chosen to attend formal schooling in post-secondary institutions, including both community college and traditional four-year bachelor degree programs.

Many mentees have gone directly into working in their area of expertise. Examples of career paths chosen include the following: musician, film director, graphic artist, computer programmer, chef, film location scout, butcher, actor, costume designer, visual artist, make-up artist, tattoo artist, and photographer. Those who have gone on to pursue bachelor degrees have been admitted to the programs of their choice by taking the appropriate prerequisites in order to enroll. This may have meant writing SAT tests, taking academic bridging programs, or by creating portfolios of their work that correspond to the academic requirements.

One of the questions people often ask when told about Alpha II is, "but how does this choice ultimately benefit them in life?" The importance of being able to tell your own story and know yourself is the most important take away from the role self-directed learning plays in approaching life. What Alpha II is able to provide is encouraging and reinforcing a healthy mental state of being that mentees can maintain throughout their life's pursuits. Alpha II provides a love of learning as well and an understanding that learning takes place everywhere, not just in a typical classroom environment.

Whatever road "graduates" of Alpha II take, as Peter Gray and Gina Riley have noted in their study of unschoolers, they have been able to successfully learn, grow, and work in relation to any career choice when they concentrate on what they personally value. And Alpha II has been an important ingredient in their continued ability to choose the learning they value for themselves.

References

Freire, P. (1981). *Pedagogy of the oppressed*: Translation by Myra Bergman Ramos from Portuguese in 1968. New York: The Continuum Publishing Corporation.

Gray, P. & Riley, G. (2013). The challenges and benefits of unschooling, according to 232 families who have chosen that route. *Journal of Unschooling and Alternative Learning, 7*(14).

Holt, J. (1964). *How children fail*. New York: Dell.

Illich, I. D. (1972). *Deschooling society*. New York: Harper & Row.

Neill, A. S. (1960). *Summerhill: A radical approach to child rearing*. New York: Hart Pub.

Provincial committee on aims and objectives of education. *Living and learning: The report of*

Carol Nash

*the provincial committee on aims and objectives
of education in the schools of
Ontario, January 1, 1968.*
https://www.connexions.org/CxLibrary/Docs/CX
5636-HallDennis.htm.
United Nations. (1948). Universal declaration of human
rights. https://www.un.org/en/about-us/universal-
declaration-of-human-rights.

Carol Nash holds a PhD in philosophy of education
from the Ontario Institute for Studies in Education
University of Toronto. She is a co-founder of Alpha II
Alternative School. Since 2012 she has been Scholar in
Residence in the History of Medicine, University of
Toronto. As a member of the Health, Arts and
Humanities Program in the Department of Psychiatry,
she founded and facilitates the weekly Health Narratives
Research Group. Carol is grateful for and would like to
acknowledge the helpful suggestions provided by a past
mentor at Alpha II, Joe Lasko, in improving this chapter.

Chapter 9

Pono: Democratic, Outdoor, Urban Education in New York City

Maysaa Bazna

Pono was founded in answer to a deep calling that manifested in me the day I became a mother. At the time my daughter was born, I had been in education for 13 years. During my years as an education professor, I visited many classrooms in schools that were selected by education departments as the best in New York City. Regardless of the recognition achieved by those classrooms, I rarely saw a spark of discovery in the eyes of the children or sensed a real connection between the children and what they were asked to do. The settings felt artificial, and the children seemed to give in to the role of being mere recipients of what they were being taught. The classrooms felt lifeless. The stark contrast between the utter joy I saw in the eyes of my daughter unraveling the world day by day and the sad boredom that I sensed in the eyes of those children cemented my concerns about the way we were schooling our children. I had lectured about how our current education system was failing our children and how we needed to do education differently. But, after my child was born, this came too close to home. That was when Pono was born. The name reflects the traditional Hawaiian concept denoting harmony and equilibrium.

The Beginning

When Pono first began, we simply provided a loving, peaceful space for our children to be, and we intentionally left the rest for them to mold. All I wanted for my daughter and other children was a place where their innate genius, curiosity, wonderment, and unbeatable desire to explore and grow would be protected. A place where children are trusted to initiate and direct their own learning in pursuit of their own happiness, and where there is no limit to what they can or want to become.

Since then, it's been the children's brilliant minds and bright souls who have shaped who we are and what we offer. We became an outdoor program when they asked for more hikes and playtime in nature. We became an urban program when their varied interests took us to many different locations in and around New York City. We increased the days of attendance gradually as they asked for more time with Pono. We became an open space with only a stage, drums, and flowers—no desks and no chairs because they asked. The structures of our daily schedules, lessons, and the different learning opportunities were designed based on the requests of the children.

Recently, when the topic of needing more space came up, the children exploded in excitement with ideas such as Pono owning its own subway car, boat, or airplane! Even though such ideas stretch the imagination of the adults quite a bit, it is quite possible that this would be the next step in the development of Pono.

The purpose of this chapter is to provide an introduction to the main elements that frame Pono's approach to learning. Along with the learner-centered educational programs out there, I hope that it inspires the creation of more such programs and that, in turn, they all serve to challenge the prevalent way of schooling children.

Every Child Has A Voice

Every child at Pono has a voice in their learning. The children, as young as two years old, design the curriculum. They initiate, direct, and regulate their learning in the manner that they choose, at their own place and pace, and for as long as they want and need. Curriculum design at Pono starts with the Interests Meeting. This is a meeting where all of the children gather to hear the interests of each other. It results in a complete plan of lessons taught by our faculty, lessons taught by visiting teachers, short and long trips, daylong trips, mentorships, and focus studies. For children to share openly their interests they needed to trust that their interests are respected by the adults and children alike. And, no matter how impossible the interests sound, we work on making them happen.

Pono's curriculum design honors the individuality of the child within a community of learners. It takes into account the learning interests of the majority of the students in class while at the same time ensuring that the decided-on lessons, trips and so on reflect at least 70% of the interests of every student in that class. The process is repeated four times a year. In the context of a year-round school calendar, it ensures that learning is dynamic, flexible, adaptive, and adjusting regularly to the interests of the students.

The curriculum design process is broken into steps that are carried out, to different degrees that correspond to their ages, by the children. The excitement exhibited by the children during planning time, as they are making all of the decisions, is a testament to the strong sense of ownership they take for their learning. The curriculum design process alone can't ensure a fulfilling child-centered learning experience. Certain elements in the learning environment are needed to ensure such an experience. At Pono, there are no tests, no grades, no homework, no compulsory lessons, and policy changes are to be approved in school meetings, as is the case in most democratic schools (Levine, 2002; Mercogliano, 1998, 2006; Mintz, 2016: Morrison, 2007). Just as learning is real, projects are real too. For example, learning math at Pono starts in cooking lessons or in making our own hand sanitizers. It can develop into running Pono's Etsy store or managing the money aspect in our fundraising events.

We offer small and individual classes in math and literacy, which allow the children to process academic subjects at their own pace; not constrained by the age or readiness of the other children in their class. For instance, a three-year-old who was reading at a second-grade level joined the literacy classes of the six and seven-year-olds. She spent the rest of the day with the other three-year-olds in her class. When a child's interest is a topic in which none of our faculty is knowledgeable, we invite a visiting teacher to work with the children. You can imagine the value of the experience for one of our children, who is fascinated with bridges, when we invited an award-winning bridge engineer to come to Pono and talk with the children about the bridges he had designed.

For a child-centered learning experience to be fulfilling, there also needs to be an established foundation of safety (Mercogliano, 2004). There is a wall in our space that is dedicated to "Pono Agreements." On that wall, it says, "We speak and act kindly with one another. If there is an act of unkindness, we call a council meeting." It also says, "A group of us go on a trip only when everyone is included." Values, principles, and agreements create the foundation of safety needed in any learner-centered program.

Each child at Pono has a voice. Not only in decisions that affect the educational program but also, more importantly, in decisions that affect how we maintain the kind, respectful, and inclusive environment that Pono is. The "Pono Agreements" wall had nothing written on it when Pono started. The main source of the agreements on the wall are council meetings. Children as young as four- and five-years-old participate in council meetings. For that age group, council meetings are facilitated by adults who support the children in generating their own solutions to a conflict. By the age of seven or eight, the children are running these council meetings with only a little help from the adults.

Children and Nature Connect

The first group of Pono children, as young as two- and three-years old, where the ones who repeatedly said, "walking in the woods" whenever asked about their interests until "walking in the woods" became an essential part of Pono.

Children are born with an intrinsic connection to nature, but often this connection is lost if it is neglected. Inner-city kids are in most need for opportunities to deepen, or sometimes rediscover, their connection to nature (Suzuki, 2007). The children's interest in shearing took us to an alpaca farm, their fascination with wolves took us to a wolf sanctuary, their questions about bee queens took us to a bee farm where they saw the queen. Their curiosities for the natural world are endless; they often request to visit nature reserves, urban farms, salt marshes, parks, animal shelters, beaches, and many other destinations in nature.

In addition to those destinations, every week, the children visit our partner sanctuary in Westchester County. There, they get to engage in the magic of nature and witness the beauty of the changing seasons. Guided by the questions the children have requested, the naturalist accompanies the children on ample experiences—whether it is catching frogs and tadpoles, walking on the iced pond, pulling castle-like creations of frozen soil from the ground, touching a blue jay that was in the bird banding net, tapping trees to make maple syrup, observing the behavior of Skittles and Houdini, the sanctuaries rabbits, or simply going on a hike. All of these activities foster a sense of empathy for nature that goes beyond anything that can be taught inside the classroom.

Chapter 9

According to the naturalist who has been working with our children at the sanctuary, Pono children, when compared to children who visit the sanctuary on a less frequent basis, are more understanding of the uniqueness of a discovery in the sanctuary's ecosystem. They express joy and wonderment for the little magical things that often go unnoticed or are commonly seen as unimportant. We find that the mysterious beauty of nature uplifts the children and deepens their connection with all living things.

Their engagement in nature is not limited to the two outdoor days a week. During indoor days, children sometimes choose to spend the whole day in the park across the street from our space happily playing, eating, jumping in rain puddles, and so on. Also, during indoor days, our children regularly visit our partner urban farms and partner gardens in Harlem. They carry out various responsibilities there, including watering, weeding, harvesting, gardening, and composting. They play, marvel at how big the cucumbers they planted are, and how delicious the cherry tomatoes taste, and simply enjoy the beauty of these oases in the middle of the hustle of the City. We have noticed that their appreciation of nature grows along with their understanding of the role they play in maintaining it.

Over the years, we have witnessed the healing effect nature has on our children. I would never forget how adamant one of our newly enrolled children was at renewing his group's mentorship with our partner sanctuary. His peers suggested doing something else since they had completed a whole year of mentorship there. In that conversation, he was no longer soft-spoken or afraid of insects. He demanded another year of mentorship, declaring that before he started going there with Pono, he had "never seen anything like that in my life." He was 10-years-old at that time. Nature has the power to rekindle that sense of wonder and excitement we all are born with and engender a feeling of peace and harmony with all other forms of life.

Children and The World Connect

Learning happens everywhere, and it happens best when children are immersed in authentic environments and situations, rather than in rigid artificial settings. At Pono, learning happens at museums, factories, wood shops, theaters, tech companies, restaurants, galleries, sports arenas, science labs, studios, a variety of traditional as well as innovative businesses, and so on. We create partnerships with different educational and cultural organizations to provide and facilitate regular access to different events and resources, and we take full advantage of the riches and resources available in New York City and the surrounding states.

Our children go on two or three trips a week. Every year, our younger children go on over 70 trips. Our older children can go on anywhere between 70 and 115 trips within New York City, depending on their selected mentorship for the term. This includes four daylong trips outside the City and one international trip. The first group of Pono students have been on over 750 trips with Pono. While they are only 12, they have seen much more of New York than I have in the 23 years I have lived here.

Daylong trips are to deepen the children's understanding of a topic they have been studying, beyond what NYC offers. For example, after they studied the constitutional law for a term and visited all relevant locations in NYC, we took them on a daylong trip to Philadelphia. They visited the most historic sites in America's birthplace, including the Liberty Bell and Independence Hall. They also visited a nonprofit, nonpartisan institution devoted to the United States Constitution. There, they attended a multimedia theatrical production titled *Freedom Rising,* visited an interactive exhibit on the story of "We The People," and toured an iconic hall with 42 life-size bronze statues of the Founding Fathers.

International trips are designed to answer a question the children have been studying beyond what New York and its neighboring states offer. Studying biodiversity and sustainability took us to Costa Rica. In addition to the educational aspects of the trip, the students had the opportunity to connect with Costa Rica's local communities. The experience helped strengthen their compassion for others and further deepened their understanding of the world. As one of the Pono students puts it,

> Sometimes I feel that there are too many people in the world who do not understand, respect, and accept people whose lives are different than theirs. A powerful way to remedy this is travel; to explore and learn about people's lives, cultures,

and traditions and really make an effort to connect.

Children and Knowledge Connect

In addition to the lessons offered by our faculty and the tours given by guides on field trips, Pono offers more than 450 lessons a year taught by visiting teachers. We do this to expand our student's experience beyond our faculty's expertise and knowledge, and to connect them with professionals and educators in the community who share their interests. Our very long list of visiting teachers is as diverse as the children's interests, and it has included award-winning authors, engineers, college professors, dancers, activists, chefs, paleontologists, mime artists, sports coaches, historians, inventors, geologists, musicians, wood workers, fashion designers, and many more. Finding visiting teachers is as equally challenging as it is rewarding for the adults at Pono. However, the perspectives that these individuals share is of immeasurable value.

When a visiting teacher stands the test of the children's inquisitive minds, the children request that they come back for another lesson. When the request is repeated over and over again, they end up visiting regularly. This is how Pono came to have regular visiting teachers in science, art, music, Greek mythology, meditation, wrestling, coding, and other subjects.

Children and Pono Connect

Chapter 9

The role of teachers at Pono is of paramount importance. They are individuals who cherish the brilliance and beaming curiosity of the children they support, honoring their interests and natural development. More importantly, they nurture the children's intrinsic humanity and wisdom as they accompany the children on a journey to becoming balanced human beings. They teach by example how to be socially conscious, and how to live harmoniously in a community where one's freedom ends when it interferes with the freedom of others (Neill, 1966).

Another aspect that is essential to nurturing the heart is play. Children are immersed in an environment that values play for all ages. We appreciate play in which the child is the initiator, actor, and director (Gerber, 2003), not play-based learning or learning-based play. We practice natural, original play with our children that shows love, compassion, and kindness. Original play helps strengthen the children's wellbeing by recognizing, strengthening, and nurturing qualities that are inherent in us (Donaldson, 1993). Over the years, we have witnessed how play creates feelings of safety, trust, belonging, and connection that go beyond age, language, culture, and abilities. We have also witnessed how feeling loved, respected, and safe are the foundations for optimal neurodevelopment and learning.

Children and the Future Connect

For the past 10 years, we trusted the children to know what they wanted to learn and how far they wanted

169

to pursue their learning journeys. They consistently surpassed our constantly increasing expectations. As young as five, they decided to study entomology, baking, geology, theater, and chemistry, among other topics. Also, as young as five, they wrote the script of their own musical, in which they sang, acted, and co-directed.

When the children requested to dig deeper into an area of study, we began to offer weekly classes that provided an in-depth examination of the chosen topic. These are now regular structures that we call "Focus Studies." Focus studies are offered for a whole term. Some focus studies get to develop into a project; in other words, they turn into a mentorship because the engagement of the children takes us there. Mentorships are longer in-depth explorations during which a mentor guides the children. They may last for one term or up to two years, depending on the selected topic and the scale of the project the children decide to produce.

Children ages seven to ten wrote and illustrated *The Earthsavers*, an eight-chapter comic book about six superheroes, each based on one of the children, who work together to save the Earth from volcanic eruptions and earthquakes caused by drilling companies (Hatab et al., 2017). The book celebrates individuality while also highlighting the power of working as a group. *The Earthsavers* was published and is being sold at major bookstores in New York City. When the book was first released, the children held book readings and signed the books of those who attended. Later, they turned the book into a musical in which they acted, sang, and created the set. Throughout this mentorship, which lasted for two years, the children worked with three mentors: a literacy specialist who also has a background in theatre, an artist, and a musician.

In another example, children as young as seven to nine years old were concerned about whether Donald Trump's travel ban in 2016 was legal and decided to better understand the powers of the president. They chose constitutional law to be their focus study. The immigration law attorney who led this focus study introduced them to the concepts of federalism, separation of powers, the Bill of Rights, and others. The children's examination of constitutional law led to a project. They wanted to know how children their age in Harlem felt about the current presidency. To this goal, and under the mentorship of a researcher, they wrote a survey and administered it to over 400 children. They analyzed the data, wrote the report, and presented their survey findings at an international education conference in Long Island. Later, the children requested to learn more about civil disobedience and activism. Their examination of civil rights movements in a follow-up focus study culminated in a protest alongside of activists against deportation and support of immigrants' rights. This learning journey was filmed as a short documentary titled, *We The Children,* which was screened at 11 film festivals in New York, Los Angeles, Canada, and Greece and won four awards. The children attended many of these screenings and participated in post-screening Q&As.

The children are showing brilliant academic performance, but more importantly, they are confident and comfortable in their immediate and expansive community. They approach life with minds and spirits that are readily engaged. They see themselves as active creators of their future, not passive recipients. They are deeply connected with nature. They are loving and caring, and it is truly a pleasure being around them.

In Pursuit of Happiness

A friend of mine, who knew that Sulaf, my daughter and the first student enrolled in Pono, was writing a chapter in this book about her Pono experience (see chapter 12), wondered how I would handle the process. She asked whether we would write together and discuss our ideas along the way or write separately, and, whether I would ask her to make any changes to parts that I didn't like. I didn't know the answer, and I definitely felt the burden of the question. But I didn't need to live with that burden for long because it quickly occurred to me what I should do. I'd do what we always did at Pono when decisions about the children need to be made. I'd ask the children!

When I asked my daughter, she said she wanted us to write separately, that she didn't want to read my chapter as I was writing it, and that she might or might not read hers to me before sending it to the editors. A couple of days before the chapter was due, and out of the blue, Sulaf started reading her chapter to me. We both burst out in laughter at the stories she wrote. She neither asked me if she should change anything, nor did I suggest that she should.

Happiness wraps itself around everyone when the simple basic concept of democratic education is exercised. When we trust children to initiate and direct their learning, they will guide the way, and they will get there. The world will be a much better place when all children have the right to be active participants in their education and have a voice in decisions that affect them.

References

Donaldson, O.F. (1993). *Paying by heart: The vision and practice of belonging*. Arlington, VA: Health Communications Inc.

Gerber, M. (2003). *Dear parent: Caring for infants with respect* (2nd edition). Los Angeles, CA: Resources for Infant Educators (RIE).

Hatab., S., Mikami, T. M., Narciso, C., Narciso, M., Halpert, A. R., & Stoneberg, J. (2017) *The earthsavers*. New York, NY: Pono Center Inc.

Levine, E. (2002). *One kid at a Time: Big lessons from a small school*. New York, NY: Teachers College Press.

Mercogliano, C. (1998). *Making it up as we go along: The story of the Albany Free School*. Portsmouth, NH: Heinemann.

Mercogliano , C. (2004). *A school must have a heart: And other essays on education*. Oxford, NY: The Oxford Village Press.

Mercogliano, C. (2006). *How to grow a school: Starting and sustaining schools that work*. Oxford, NY: The Oxford Village Press.

Mintz, J. (2016). *School's over: How to have freedom and democracy in education*. Roslyn Heights,

NY: Alternative Education Resources Organization.

Morrison, K. A. (2007). *Free school teaching: A Journey into radical progressive education.* Albany, NY: State University of New York Press.

Neill, A. S. (1966). *Freedom—not license!* New York, NY: Hart Publishing company.

Suzuki, D (2007). *Sacred balance: Rediscovering our place in nature.* Vancouver, Canada: Greystone Books Ltd.

Maysaa Bazna is an avid advocate for equity and inclusion in education. Her mission is to support learning programs where children have a voice in their education and to help cultivate children's intrinsic humanity and wisdom for a more just and harmonious world. She directs the Office of Clinical Practice at the School of Education of Queens College, CUNY, where equity, excellence, and ethics are the core values that guide the experiences of future teachers. She also runs Friends of Pono, a not-for-profit organization that supports and advances learner-centered environmental education programs in NYC public schools.

Chapter 10

The Pathfinder Community School

Hope Wilder

Walking into Pathfinder, you are greeted by piles of shoes outside the columned door. The sidewalk has colorful hopscotch boards, some of which go as high as 76, some which have wiggly annotated obstacle courses. Tires lie around in the yard which has a swing set, a large barrel, and a community garden. Children roam freely throughout the campus. Inside, there is a looping corridor of rooms, including a Rumpus Room, Music Room, Computer room, and more. The unique thing about Pathfinder is that all of these features were designed, requested, and voted for approval by the twenty or so 5- to 14-year-olds who form the community.

Pathfinder is a self-directed and self-governing community where every voice is heard. It is a daytime village for children where they are free to create their own worlds and do almost anything they put their minds to. It can at times seem like a chaotic place where no "education" happens. We call it "Real Life Learning" for a reason—kids learn everything here from how to tie a shoe, how to operate a microwave, how to stand up for what you believe in, how to collaborate and work with others, to how to deal with heartbreak. We make space for kids to fully experience the wonderful joy of making a best friend for the first time, or alternatively to experience the unbearable pain of losing a best friend for the first time. Pushing themselves to achieve big goals,

175

they fail. It is a very intense curriculum when you look at it that way.

Pathfinder was founded in 2016 in Durham, NC as a self-directed learning community. Registered homeschoolers attend from 3-5 days a week on a sliding scale membership fee that accommodates a diverse range of incomes. The children are called "members" rather than students or learners to reflect our commitment to true self-direction, as we don't see a tidy division between adults as "teachers" and children as "students," we believe that learning can happen in any direction. We also use the word "member" to underscore the responsibility that signing a membership agreement brings.

Our approach combines elements of self-directed education, democratic free schools, and Agile Learning Center tools. Because of a strong commitment to consent and member participation, we also use a consent based governance system that originated in the Netherlands called Sociocracy. Our justice system is based on conflict resolution skills, mediation, and restorative justice practices. In what follows, I will describe how we incorporate each of these structures, and how they support and reinforce our core values of freedom and consent. We say that "community is our curriculum," and in that sense the following is our core curriculum at Pathfinder.

Self-Directed Education

The core of our program is self-directed education. What that means at Pathfinder is a consent-

176

based approach, grounded in trust that learning is happening all the time. Members are free to opt out of anything that is happening, other than the core community participation requirements of clean-up time, democratic meetings, and conflict resolution.

On a day to day basis, self-directed education looks like play. We believe that play is important and educational work for children, and I have seen play lead to learning time and time again with our members. The hopscotch boards that loop around the sidewalk allow opportunity for balance, coordination, and practicing numbers. Creating games together requires intense learning of social/emotional skills, communication, and collaboration. Our children speak almost non-stop all day to each other, developing their verbal acumen at light speed, learning vocabulary and expression through the art of conversation with people of all ages. Our members create new worlds through imagination on a daily basis, and play creates the scaffolding for learning through living.

Democratic Free School Inspiration

Pathfinder was initially inspired by Sudbury schools and other democratic free schools founded in the 1960s like Albany Free School, as well as Summerhill in England. Pathfinder shares similarities with democratic free schools including our Bill of Rights for children in our space, participatory democracy, and a participatory justice system. The members have the legally protected right to choose their activities, the right to a clean and safe environment, the right to privacy, and the right to peaceably exist in our space free from forced curriculum. These rights come with responsibilities and expectations of our members, and our staff is there to guide members as they learn how to uphold them. These rights are so central to our philosophy that we incorporated them into our corporate bylaws.

However, there are distinct differences to the Pathfinder model, we don't have a Lawbook but instead have four Agreements—Respect Self and Others, Take Care of Stuff and People, Participate, and Help Solve Conflicts. Weekly meetings are held to come up with or change new Practices that help us uphold these four agreements that members sign on to when they come into the community. There are about a dozen or so "rules" that connect to the four Agreements including the following: Be Appropriate, Clean Up After Yourself, and A Stop Rule.

Agile Learning Center Tools

We use tools from Agile Learning Centers including a weekly Change Up meeting to try out new practices tied to the four Agreements. Practices are written on sticky notes, tried out for two weeks, and evaluated. Any given Practice can be changed, dropped, or adopted using a consent process where everyone says they can work with the decision for a week. Adults are ultimately in charge of in the moment safety calls for legal and liability *reasons (though I can't remember how many times I've said, "It's your body, it's your choice" when a child asks me to approve their risky play!"),* however our consent-based decision making process

178

asks, "Is it good enough for now? Is it safe enough to try?" For example, the kids wanted to run in the hallways. The staff members thought it would be too dangerous, but agreed to try the practice "Run Carefully" for just one day. The next day, we asked, "Was anyone injured? Were people still able to peaceably exist?" It turned out that nobody was injured, and the kids felt safer being able to move the way they wanted to. (And move freely they do—skipping, slithering, sliding, crab-walking—their ingenuity in the art of movement continues to amaze me!) However, chasing games were inevitably too loud and too fast for safety, so the group agreed to adopt a new practice of "Chasing Games Outside Only" that still exists today. To this date we've only had one injury during indoor running play.

Another Agile Learning Center practice we use is Spawn Groups. These daily breakout groups answer questions about the community, and give same-age children a place to play and connect together with people who might not be in their social group. Spawns also elect representatives to the Members Circle which makes decisions about member finances, field trips, etc. Spawns are asked questions such as, "What makes you feel respected?" as well as "What classes and workshops would you like to see at Pathfinder?" Staff listen carefully and note down member requests, as we actively gather input and feedback from the community so we can best meet their needs. If supplies are needed for a member request, they can apply for a portion of a small program budget allowance available to the kids (their "Fun Money"), and the expenditure is voted on through Member's Circle. Workshops that require more materials or staff are offered on a sign-up board. If enough members sign up, the supplies are procured and the staff dedicate time to offer the workshop. Examples of workshops include, Slime-Making Workshop, Watercolor Painting, Clay Building, PH Experiments, Microscope Workshop, Lego Building Engineering Challenges.

Sociocracy—Consent Based Decision Making and Circle Structure

Sociocracy is a democratic governance model that has its origins in a free school in the Netherlands started by Quakers in the 1920s called De Werkplaats Kindergemeenshap. The model is based on consent, feedback loops, clarity, and transparency in decision making. A fundamental goal of the system is for everyone's voices to be heard, and everyone's needs to be met. To do that, Pathfinder is divided into "circles," which make decisions by consent. Each Circle has a clearly defined membership, domain, and aims to follow.

We currently have a Board of Directors, Parents Circle, Members Circle, Staff Circle, and a central Community Circle. The Board is in charge of mission/vision and long term planning. Parents Circle helps organize the parents to support Pathfinder and also to give feedback to the program. Members Circle is the kids, their concerns, and the focus of the program we provide. Staff Circle is in charge of running the program on a day to day basis, as well as business operations, finances, and making HR decisions. The central Community Circle is made up of two representatives from the Parents, Staff, and Members Circles, and they coordinate the whole community and facilitate communication between the other Circles. Community Circle also elects a representative of the community to the Board. It is possible (and has happened) that a member—a kid—can be elected to the board.

Consent decision making means that at every level of the organization, we make decisions in the same way. The question is, "Can I work with this decision?" and decisions have a timeline for evaluation. If someone has an objection, the group tries to work the person's concern into the decision, to make it stronger, narrower, or more complete—an even better decision that works for everyone. The beauty of the sociocratic system is that decisions are moved on quickly, and there is a sense of safety in knowing that we will return to the decision and have the opportunity to change it.

Conflict

Conflict happens when people come together in community. At Pathfinder, the first step to "Help Solve Conflicts" is to speak to the person involved. We have a worksheet that helps kids make requests of each other using Non-Violent Communication if they need help communicating clearly.

Mediation

If a conflict can't be resolved between the people involved, we ask the concerned members to participate in a mediation with a staff person. Staff have been trained in mediation techniques, and while we have offered peer mediation certification, that program is mostly aspirational at this point. We would love to get to a point where kids are taking turns helping other kids resolve conflicts.

Restorative Justice

In case mediation still does not resolve a conflict, we have a restorative practice called Culture Committee. Culture Committee is a large group mediation, facilitated by staff, that offers everyone a turn to share their point of view on what happened, their feelings about what happened, and what they need to make things better, as well as requests for the future. There are no punitive or disciplinary consequences, only "repairs" that are offered by one party to another to make things as right as possible, right now. Very often we end with signed agreements for the future.

Using this three-part conflict system, we have had enormous success keeping the peace and setting community standards. There are children who had major conflicts—to the point of bullying—who have become close friends after repeated and patient mediations.

For our community standards, very often, discussions in Culture Committee lead to ideas and practices that we then ask everyone to consent to. For instance, the agreement "Be Appropriate" has gone to many Culture Committees for interpretation. Suggestions for new practices for appropriateness came out of these discussions, such as, "Nobody wants to see underwear," or "Everyone must wear shirts, regardless of gender or age." A broad and detailed proposal defining appropriate language came out of a Culture Committee where one member was offended by the repeated use of the word "crap" by another member. Profound societal questions are discussed, such as, what is the line between self-expression and profanity? Where do we as a community draw the line for hate speech? These questions arose from Culture Committee and were discussed in Spawns to be voted on for policy in the Member's Circle. In all cases, it is the kids who are setting standards and limits for what they want at Pathfinder. Staff are allowed to voice objections that the kids then consider, but unless it is a health and safety call, the staff does not dictate terms.

We have found that the children adopt these mediation and governance practices readily, but it has been more difficult to try to engage them with the parents. However, we have recently undergone a whole-community mediation using outside facilitators but following the same structure and practices as we use with the children. We are still learning how to be effective communicators and to resolve conflicts as adults. At least for me, it's extremely hard to go up to someone you have a disagreement with and talk to them directly! By "walking the walk" as well as "talking the talk," we aim to have integrity in our program, though it is a very difficult road. Each aspect of the Pathfinder program, from our pedagogical philosophy to our restorative justice practice, connects to and reinforces the others, and they are all grounded in our foundational values of respecting children as people and operating with the consent of the governed.

In our community, self-directed learning takes many forms. Members can participate in Offerings, Workshops, and community activities, from our sociocratic governance to suggesting purchases using the Member's Circle budget. They can choose to play, start their own businesses, or make a spontaneous dance party happen. Math, reading, and other "core skills" happen as by-products of activities that are chosen by the children, with or without staff assistance, but always internally directed, sometimes with intense focus and amazing outcomes.

Candy Machines and Snack Store

One of the first member businesses has its origins in self-directed play. An 8-year-old girl who we'll call Laura would bring in bags of candy and share them with her friends. The game evolved from using a "cash register" to take toy money for candy, to giving high fives. Laura would spend ten or fifteen minutes with "candy store workers" arranging the candy by size, shape, color, or kind, and then "customers" would line up to buy candy for high fives. Laura was simply playing a game, and sharing her love of candy with her friends.

One day, Laura decided to purchase a candy machine with a loan from her mom, and to sell candy at Pathfinder for a quarter. She had to go through Member's Circle and get consent from the group—we asked the kids to give a thumbs up, (yes!), down (no, or I have an objection) or sideways (I don't really know, or I don't care). Some kids responded with some thumbs down votes. When asked about their concerns, the kids shared that they were worried about kids eating too much sugar, and not having healthy options for kids who don't eat candy. Eventually a proposal came out of this objection: to purchase a candy machine with the members' Fun Money, and to stock it with healthy options such as pistachios and almonds.

Laura got her approval of consent from all the members once these concerns were addressed. We tried out the candy machines, and indeed, kids did indeed bring in bags of quarters to buy as much candy as they could. All of a sudden, quarters were worth their weight in gold. Other kid businesses sprung up to help kids boost their own candy machine budget. There were lemonade stands, handicrafts, rainbow loom bracelets, and knitted goods. Kids would walk into our administrator, Reuben's office with handfuls of pennies or nickels and other loose change dug up from their couch cushions, and he would ask them to count out $0.25 at a time. By now, kids of all ages are much better at counting change than before!

Along the way, Laura was learning important business skills and math by calculating her initial investment, profit margins, and keeping track of sales in bags of quarters when she emptied the machines.

Eventually the candy craze died out. Through the Change-Up process, the members decided to limit the amount of candy to one small Dixie cup at a time to prevent sugar highs and mood crashes that were affecting the community. Laura reports that sales are way down, as the novelty has died out and everyone is self-regulating. (Either that or they ran out of quarters at home.)

Hope Wilder

Snack Store

At some point, one of the kids brought up in an all-group meeting that not all kids have spare money to spend on candy or almonds, and that some kids got hungry after eating all of their lunches. To help "take care of people," the kids voted to spend Member's Circle money on a monthly free snack budget, which they called Snack Store. Snack Store included Laura who had started the candy machine craze, and she lent her business acumen to the venture. The Snack Store Committee interviewed members to find out what snacks were most popular, and they spent $50 for an initial month's worth of snacks. One member asked for a print out of our attendance sheet to track who got which snack (a job that requires reading and writing skills.)

Snacks had to be counted and distributed, made sure to last the whole month. Snack Store Committee decided on rules for distributing the snacks, such as, no stealing, stand in line, and one snack per person per week. Snacks were labeled with kids' initials so that everyone would know who was responsible for wrappers left out.

Every week, the kids would line up excitedly for Snack Store. Running the store required notifying everyone, setting out the snacks, keeping track of the snack orders, and helping keep the line tidy. Snack Store ran like a well-oiled machine, much to the enjoyment of all.

After 2 months of Snack Store, the committee lost interest in tracking snacks or buying new ones. The responsibility was getting old. Because of our consent-based processes, the Snack Store committee was allowed to dissolve, and so far nobody has stepped up to revive the practice.

The story of Candy Store and Snack Store follows a now-familiar arc: someone comes up with an idea that has momentum, and spreads like wildfire. There is initial excitement and great participation. The new phenomenon takes time to settle into a steady pattern, then runs as a steady state for several weeks. At some point, people lose interest and there are residual leftovers from the craze, and long-term hiccups of nostalgia for the way things used to be. Then a new idea springs up. Last week, it was crocheting that took over the community. Next week, who knows?

A common concern from parents is that their children will not learn reading or math. As you can see from the previous story, math is woven into our program in such a way that children are exposed to numbers all the time. They can take it or leave it, but they know that if they want to, they can step into a role of responsibility with spending money, and they get remarkably good at estimating costs for their budget.

As for reading, our environment is intensely verbal and a lot of important information is to be found in writing. Rules for rooms are posted on the door, (for example, No Eating in the Music Room) and daily activities are written on sticky notes for our big whiteboard calendar and everyone's names appear again and again in Spawn lists, sign-ups for workshops and field trips, certifications, chore checking, and more. We have a library—which is the protected quiet room—full of books, comics, easy readers, and graphic novels. I have seen kids go from reading the alphabet to sounding out easy readers to devouring *Calvin and Hobbes* in a few months.

One way they learn reading skills is by being elected Chore Checker. Chore Checkers make sure everyone does their chore at the end of the day, and checks off their name on a list. Often the youngest members are elected, and they stand tall with pride for the responsibility they carry to safeguard our common space from dirt and germs. It's a requirement to at least know which letter each person's name starts with to check them off. Often kids learn to read by starting with their friends' names.

Learning to read happens in more traditional ways as well. One young member requested Spelling Workshops, and a staff member made time to sit with him and play Junior Scrabble, essentially a spelling game. Another time, a local bookseller dropped off a bunch of early release books they had been sent for review. The kids took checking out the books to review them very seriously. One mother shared with me that she had never seen her daughter read a book for fun before, due to having been scarred in her previous schooling by being labeled "behind" the class for her natural learning pace. The member came up to me glowing with pride the next day, and told me it had been a very good book. She read it in one night!

Video Games to Software Engineer

Our first "graduate" spent most of his time at Pathfinder on computers, either playing Minecraft or coding in the Minecraft world. After a short time, I realized that he knew more about computers than any of the staff, so I arranged an internship for him at a local software company. In 6 months, he learned 3 programming languages, and started participating in the international open source community as a contributor. I would see him scribbling in algebra on whiteboards to work out some coding problem he was working on. He absorbed coding through being in an environment with experienced practitioners who shared the same interests, and by asking questions when he got stuck doing research on his own. Now, he is the one offering advice to professionals at age 15 because he had the free time to learn over 6 programming languages!

I am continually amazed to see the learning and development that happens when children are free to explore a rich and stimulating environment, full of caring people and fun things to do. I truly believe that learning is natural, it happens all the time.

I founded Pathfinder because I wanted a place where I could be free to be a person among children, where we could treat each other as people, not "teacher" and "student." There is nothing so freeing as being able to converse with a child about any topic they choose.

I am a former science and naturalist teacher, and I have gone through a journey regarding classes, workshops, and offerings. When I first started working in a self-directed environment, I remember thinking, "I have so much to offer the children because of my teaching experience!" I would offer "cool" workshops that used to be a favorite when I was teaching in an environment where the kids had to pay attention to my lesson plan. In a self-directed environment, kids would drift by, play with the microscope for a few minutes, and drift on. I had to learn to let go of understanding "teaching" as only formal classes, and it was humbling to see how little help the children "needed" from me to learn something when left to their own devices.

After I got over the blow to my instructor's ego, I was able to observe the many different ways that the kids do value adults in our program. Many children thrive on adult attention, and while we do try to "wean" the kids from having one adult focused on them all the time, our staff are expected to maintain mentoring relationships with kids. I love listening to kid stories, and hearing all the latest in make-believe. Our program is founded on the quality of relationships between all of the community members—adults and children alike.

Children see the adults around them as resources. We keep things running, in concrete, material ways. If art supplies run out, or there is a mess, the staff help out. We help with band-aids, with teaching kids how to tie their shoes, with certifications. Certifications are required for kids to be able to use equipment that needs safety instruction, such as the toaster, microwave, tea kettle, and the Internet. Sometimes I am exhausted by all the requests and interruptions, and feel that my entire job is replacing tape rolls and picking up tiny stray socks!

But children also see staff as resources to learn about the world of ideas. One time I was sitting at the lunch table in the "eating zone" and someone asked me a question out of the blue about acids and bases. I dusted off my chemistry knowledge and gave a brief explanation of how acids and bases react to form water and salts. I helped the kids look online for more information, and they learned that baking soda and vinegar also create CO2, which results in the bubbling.

I have had long conversations with our resident astrophysics geek about gas planets versus terrestrial ones, the latest astronomical discoveries, the origins of the universe, theories of dark matter, and the probable end of the Cosmos. Conversations happen spontaneously, and can go anywhere! Learning also happens in multiple directions—whoever has the sufficient knowledge to answer a question as it arises offers what they know, serendipitous timing for learning and connecting.

Kids love to geek out with the adults about shared interests. The fantasy fans gravitate towards the staff who like Dungeons & Dragons, the anime kids gravitate towards the staff who like anime. The outdoorsy and nature-loving kids gravitate towards me, as I am pretty much always down to go off-trail in the woods, or flip over a log and catch some invertebrates for fun. We wander through the woods together and map out all the best places to slide down rock waterslides in the creek, or to find wild mulberries and honeysuckle.

I treasure the moments when I can simply connect over a shared experience, interest, or hobby. The same joy I feel when connecting to people of all ages bubbles up in me.

The most magical moments for me have involved transcendent spontaneous events that emerge and arise, like magic. Dance parties and jam sessions arise in the corridors when our most musical member is present, each time bearing a different instrument. Once I was playing cello in the yard on a beautiful late spring day, just for my own pleasure. Earlier I had offered a "cello petting zoo" where kids could play with the strings or bang on the cello for fun. I was just playing for myself when one young member started dancing, free-form and improvisationally in the yard. We spoke a common language of free expression as I watched her closely to improvise music to accompany her dance, and she responded to my music with her self-expression. Afterward, she told me that she was "dancing the way she felt inside," and I said, "Me too."

The process of founding Pathfinder and keeping it running for the first two years has been by far the most challenging, surprising, exhausting, and worthwhile venture I have ever embarked on. Every day is an adventure, and it's not at all easy. We've had many mishaps and ups and downs, some of which have nothing to do with self-directed education but simply with running a business. Our basement space has flooded, the water has been turned off, glass windows have been broken, and furniture worn out. We've dealt with angry parents, difficult staff, and we've sanitized the space from floor to ceiling countless times.

But whenever I see a child slithering down the hallway like a snake, using a piece of furniture in a surprising and unexpected fashion, or when I see the pure joy on someone's face as they bond with new friends, I feel that it has all been worthwhile. I get to see children grow into themselves as they try on new identities through play. I am privileged to be a part of their lives in this alchemical formative process, and it is a beautiful thing to see unfold first-hand. Creating a space where children have the freedom to be themselves and truly belong has been an honor.

I truly believe that self-directed learning is the future of education. I am proud to be a part of a larger movement to work towards freedom for children in choosing what they learn, how they learn, and from whom they learn. I look forward to seeing these ideas spread like wildfire in the world.

Hope Wilder is a lifelong learner and community builder living in the Triangle for the past 15 years. She had an accelerated experience of the public school system, graduating from the University of South Carolina at the age of 19 with degrees in Biology and German. For the dozen years before starting Pathfinder, she worked and played as an alternative outdoor educator and science teacher at private schools and local nonprofits including Piedmont Wildlife Center and Duke Gardens. At Pathfinder, Hope loves spending time with the kids as a volunteer, along with running the website, and helping out with the PR/ Outreach and Admissions Committees. She enjoys making art & music, DIY fashion, and being outside.

Part 2: Student Approaches to Self-Directed Learning

Chapter 11

Practicing Freedom

Idzie Desmaris

I like to tell people that I'm a kindergarten drop-out. It seems to conjure an image of an irrepressible 5-year-old, with a personality too large to be contained in a classroom. What it actually meant in practice was that my quiet, watchful, rule-abiding self wasn't having an ideal experience of early schooling, and my parents decided to give homeschooling a go.

Homeschooling grew, with a loosening of expectations and the gaining of confidence, rather organically into unschooling, into a way of life that centered learning through living instead of curriculum. I have described unschooling many different ways over the years: as delight-driven, interest-based learning, as adult-supported self-directed education, or simply as life learning. But moving away from perhaps too many hyphens, I think to get to the heart of it is to describe unschooling as the practice of trusting and respecting children, believing in the innate talent humans have for learning, and then doing our best as adults to create and facilitate the types of environments and relationships that will best support children in their journey. It's replacing coercion with collaboration, seeing education not as something *done to* children, but arising instead from every aspect of a person's life. How does that work in practice, and what does it feel like to grow up this way? When I think about my childhood, so many different answers come to mind. . . .

Idzie Desmaris

Sometimes unschooling felt like a routine, a scaffolding of different happenings on different days that tied my life together. Structure is something which is brought up a lot in discussions of self-directed education. When you talk about living without a standardized, adult-enforced curriculum, without a succession of classes with clear times and transitions marked by a bell, some people take that to mean that unschoolers eschew anything that looks remotely like schooling (books or teachers or classes).

The reality, though, is much more complicated. When a learner is the main one driving their own education, they'll frequently choose to do things that involve more structure, at least some of the time.

I certainly did. I went to Sparks through Girl Guides, took French lessons, history, doll making, and a slew of other topics depending on what was available, affordable, and in line with my interests. There were generally a few topics I was especially interested in that dominated my library book selections and thoughts.

Without mandated structure, my days still had a rhythm, and the periods in my life with less of a routine I generally felt its lack. Which isn't to say that I didn't have a lot of free time—I did—but there were activities to mark my days and shape my weeks that gave some form of structure to my education, a structure that I appreciated.

Unschooling is less about how much or little a child's education looks like schooling, as that will vary greatly between individuals and families, and far more about self-direction, and choice, and consent.

Chapter 11

Sometimes unschooling felt like the focused concentration as I sat, holed up in my room, reading and re-reading a favourite poem.

We had a lot of books in the house. Shelves filled with sci-fi paperbacks from the 1980s, rows of cookbooks, math textbooks, plant identification guides, historical novels, and poetry.

I learned to read "late," according to a timeline I had no part in choosing and would never have accepted if I had been consulted, but once I got started, I never looked back. *Harry Potter* quickly got left behind in favour of Diana Wynne Jones' twisty and disturbing children's fantasy novels, various historical novels, and non-fiction about WWII. And poetry. So much poetry! Like the titular *Anne of Green Gables*, I longed to dance through wildflowers, reciting poems by Tennyson and Yeats. So I'd pick some to memorize, sometimes, and seated on the floor with a slightly musty hardcover picked up at the thrift store spread before me, I would whisper the lines over and over again, until they were etched in place, my tongue shaping words with the barest of thought.

Since even the many bookcases in our house weren't truly enough, we were at the library at least once a week. Browsing the shelves was a joy, rough carpet prickling my legs as I knelt on the floor, fingers tracing along spines until something caught my interest. When my younger sister turned five and could finally get a library card of her own, she'd max out the 50 item limit every time, and send me staggering out with some of the considerable overflow of bags that wouldn't fit on her narrow shoulders.

197

Idzie Desmaris

Language was something fun, playful, social and creative. We'd read aloud to each other from the newspaper, write our own poetry and stories, talk enthusiastically about the books we were reading. With only spotty and pretty quickly abandoned phonics instruction when I was small, I learned to truly read because I lived in a literate household where reading was valued, and I had the support of adults who cared about my wellbeing (I also didn't have any learning disabilities which might have made it a more difficult or complicated process).

Environment goes a long way in shaping education, and I lived in an environment filled with words. Sometimes, unschooling felt like boredom. I don't mean that in a negative way, just as a statement of fact, and it was an experience that quickly became part of my creative and educational process. I would sprawl out dramatically on the couch, exasperated by the perceived lack of options, and complain, until I got caught on a thought, an idea, something that sparked interest, and I'd be off writing or learning to play something new on the ukulele, or picking out a book from our home collection, or carefully stepping through the garden outside, checking on my vegetables.

I have generally seen boredom and daydreaming as kin, one slipping easily into the other, frustration turning into that space in which new ideas, new projects, and new approaches to problems are born. Living within such a loose structure, one I had the power to adjust as I desired, gave me the freedom in which I could just think for long stretches of time, more fully able to develop my thoughts than if I'd had little time that was truly my own.

Chapter 11

Which isn't to say that boredom is always such a benign force: at times, especially when it drags on too long, it can be a sign of a lack of balance, where all of your needs are not being met. It can also be a sign of depression. Both have been true for me, at different points in my life, but I still don't really view it as a negative emotion. It points towards the need for change in one way or another, whether that change is a shift to more constructive imagining or a need to seek some type of help. Either way, it often proceeds something new.

Sometimes unschooling felt like the excitement of bursting out of the car ready to hike in one of my favourite places, air suffused with the scent of pine trees and damp stone.

I tracked the passage of my weeks, my months, and my years by the turning of the seasons. The way hot summers filled with screaming cicadas and ripening fruits, ground dusty beneath small bare feet, faded into the cool evenings and scattered leaves of autumn. How the crunch of fresh snow and the muffled hush of the woods in winter melted into the cries of spring peepers and bloom of trilliums.

My family had the time, desire, and access to be outside, so that's what we did. I went on hikes, graduated from catching grasshoppers in the meadows near my great-grandmother's house to catching frogs in rush lined ponds nearer to my own home. I learned about photosynthesis and the migration of Canada Geese, that staghorn sumac made for a tasty burst of vitamin C and that jewelweed was a useful treatment for poison ivy rashes. Group hikes with other homeschoolers were common, as was skating on frozen ponds and cross-country skiing in the winter.

My sister remarked recently that one of the things she values most about her childhood is the love of nature it instilled, and I feel similarly. I've always loved the way being outside, no matter the season, seems to help my mind wander and stretch, finding previously elusive answers to problems of all different types.

As unschoolers we certainly didn't have a monopoly on outdoor exploration, but what we did have in abundance was *time*. We also had a life untethered from a school building or school schedule, free to find our unique educations in libraries and homes (ours and others), community centers and rented church basements, in parks and fields and woods, by rivers, and ponds, and the coast.

Time plus flexibility of space provided us with the room we needed to develop a depth of appreciation for the natural world, one that wasn't so readily available to many children we knew in school.

Sometimes unschooling felt like the giddy freedom of play, the solemn focus of imagination, or the uncomplicated contentment of consuming a well-loved book or film.

I think fun is more important than education, and I think many people have learned to place strict lines between the two that are unhelpful and inaccurate. I also believe how happy someone is will always be more important than what facts they know, how well they can take a test, or whether they can answer a rudely quizzing stranger (an occurrence far too common for those who don't go to school).

Chapter 11

Idleness is no crime, and my childhood was spent largely in activities that were not explicitly "educational"—you won't find frog catching on any curriculum I'm aware of—but were definitely fun.

I spent countless hours sitting on the hard laminate of my sister's bedroom floor building elaborate Playmobile villages, complete with homemade set pieces. Hours spent in wildly collaborative storytelling (also known as playing pretend). I read hundreds of novels, made countless works of art, and composed dozens of haiku. I ran and played outside, settling myself on the perfect bluff from which to watch the sunset night after night.

When you stop seeing education through the lens of schooling, how well something would fit into a curriculum doesn't matter anymore. It matters that children get to play, that they have the support they need, that they're learning to live in community with others. Things both less tangible and more meaningful than anything that could be tested.

Sometimes unschooling felt like finding the right balance of the right people, trying to create or discover a community that felt right.

Relationships form the backbone of an unschooling lifestyle. Sometimes, I think, the "self-directed" descriptor leads others to assume it's a solitary practice, every child their own mountain (or every family an isolated island unto themselves). Yet community, friendships, mentorships—relationships of all types—are essential. No one can be truly self-sufficient, and it's not something I'd ever aspire to even if I thought it was attainable. From the classes and clubs

Idzie Desmaris

I was a part of, to the time spent wandering through museums with groups of other kids, day camps at a local zoo, teachers and friends and librarians, there were countless people who became a part of my journey, contributed in ways great and small to my learning, my joy, and my wellbeing. For this lifestyle to work best, I think the ideal is to be rooted in community, to have easy access to the resources and support other people provide, in both more and less structured ways.

 I also found that the way I grew up impacted the types of relationships I formed. I didn't really learn to respect authority the way many others were taught. Not in a careless way; I was, if anything, overly careful of the spaces I inhabited and the people I interacted with. I was a reserved and polite child. But when I say I did not learn to respect authority, I mean that I never truly internalized the idea that some people were *better* than me, more important, more deserving of deference. Growing up without the hierarchies and authoritarianism experienced by many children in traditional schools led me to start asking some serious questions about hierarchy and authority, about the way power causes harm, and my experience undeniably shaped the politics I was drawn to as I grew older.

 Even when it came to adults who held the role of teachers or mentors, often it just felt like a different type of friendship. People across ages can relate to each other in mutually respectful ways, seeking both to teach and learn, a give and take that remains thoughtful and humble. I think when you make the shift to see children as people equally deserving of respect, and when children expect to have equal relationships with adults, those types of dynamics naturally start to form.

Not always, of course, and when you're living in a way that's so different from most of the people around you, it can at times be undeniably lonely. I always had numerous options for social interaction, with both other kids and adults, but I didn't always have groups I felt I fit in with, or people I felt understood me. I think that can be the case for many children regardless of education—especially when you tend towards watchful and reserved—but there is another layer of difficulty when you've careened off the well-worn path and are bushwhacking instead.

But along the way, there were still many good friendships, good groups of people, good mentors, and the feeling that I had people who cared about and understood me.

Sometimes unschooling felt like the long exhalation of relief upon letting something you've come to hate go.

When you choose what you do, you also get to choose what you DON'T do. With self-directed education comes the freedom to quit. Some moments I consider truly defining in my childhood were moments when I refused. When I said I didn't want to take piano lessons anymore, and stood firm in the face of my grandmother's disapproval, indignation hot in my chest that she thought she could control my actions or my choices (sometimes love does not come with understanding).

That didn't mean there weren't times I felt pressure—from my own parents, other adults, or peers—

to continue activities which were not a positive part of my life. There were also times I benefited from encouragement to continue difficult pursuits I was tempted to quit not because I hated them or had truly lost interest, but just because I had hit a temporary setback that I was finding difficult to overcome. I imagine finding that balance, of encouragement to work through difficulty with encouragement to let go of what no longer serves, is a difficult line to walk as a caregiver. But I remain deeply grateful for the times I was trusted to just stop doing something, to stop showing up to the dance class that was making me sick with anxiety, or reading a classic and supposedly important book that I just couldn't stand.

It gives a child confidence, that surety that they get to choose what they do with their time, what topics they bend their minds towards. It makes them feel trusted, a sense of security in their own lives. As far as I'm concerned, it's invaluable.

Sometimes unschooling felt like pulling together the various connections, knowledge and skills and experiences and feelings and goals, into a more cohesive design, stepping back (metaphorically) to view, with a certain amount of surprise, an education made whole. What does a self-directed education look like? It's something as varied as every individual, coloured by their families and communities as much as by their own unique quirks and passions. Instead of seeing this as a flaw—the idea of "gaps" in education—I see it as a strength, one which exists alongside the acknowledgement that everyone, no matter their background, has gaps. In the ocean of knowledge in which we all swim, each of us will only ever be able to learn and experience so much, and I don't believe anyone has a right to decide and dictate what every single child should know. I genuinely believe that we'd all be better off if the focus was less on making sure every child had a uniform education, and instead the focus was on helping a child grow in the ways they want to, to embrace what they most love doing, respond to the needs of their communities, and seek to work towards creating a better world.

When you unschool, education doesn't have an end-date, a finish line, a time when you're over and done. While it is the responsibility of the adults in a child's life to ensure they have adequate resources, support, and exposure, there's also always the awareness that if something isn't learned by a certain age, it can always be learned later, and will almost certainly be retained better when actively chosen. I know that my education is ongoing, that I will always be learning and changing, growing as a person and adjusting as best I can to new circumstances.

As I embark on some major life transitions, all the attitudes I cultivated growing up as an unschooler make me feel at least somewhat better able to learn what I need to know, despite the worry and uncertainty that often accompanies major change. Sometimes, unschooling just feels like life, like living, with all its complexities and difficulties. And in that light, I've never stopped doing it.

Idzie Desmarais is a grown unschooler, life learner, and unschooling advocate. Idzie is a writer and blogger, cooker, baker, and fermenter of tasty foods. Idzie is a queer-anarcha-feminist, an avid reader and watcher of fantasy and supernatural genres. Idzie is seeking the radical rural homesteading dream.

She was born, raised, and still resides in the Montreal area of Quebec, Canada. She dropped out of kindergarten (aka her parents decided homeschooling was a better idea than school), and grew up, along with her sister, learning from the world around her. What started out as very relaxed homeschooling slipped seamlessly into completely unschooling, and she never looked back.

As soon as she learned how to read, she started working her way voraciously through the children's section of the library. A love of reading gradually grew into a love of writing, and she started her blog, *I'm Unschooled. Yes, I Can Write* in 2008, combining her love of writing and unschooling. Since the start of that blog, she has written articles on unschooling and youth rights for *Life Learning Magazine*; *Home Education Magazine*; and *Our Schools, Ourselves*, as well as various other magazines and websites. She has also spoken at a slew of conferences, including the Tororto Unschooling Conference, the Northeast Unschooling Conference, The Quebec Association Of Home Based Education Symposium, Conférence l'Éducation, and Rethinking Everything.

Chapter 12

Pono From A Child's Perspective

Sulaf Hatab

Hi! You're the person I'm supposed to meet with to talk about Pono, right? Great, I'm glad I found you. I'm Sulaf Hatab, and I'm 12, if you wanted to know, and it's really nice to meet you. Is my hair okay? The wind is crazy this time of the year. I feel like a cyclone might carry me away to Oz at any time. No, it looks fine? Thank you, I've been worrying about that. Now, I'm supposed to tell you all the crazy stories I've archived from my time at Pono, right? No? Wait, you actually want me to tell you about Pono, like what it is, and the model, and stuff like that? Dang, I was really looking forward to getting those stories out in print! And I had such good stories, too— The profound mourning that occurred after the murder of Ted the Tick (Named after Ted Danson, of course); the pouring rain that soaked through our suitcases during our trip to Costa Rica; and, the mad dashes for the train in Philadelphia, Long Island, and wherever Vassar College is. Gosh, I'm so disappointed. But if you want my in-depth description of Pono so badly, then fine, I'll tell all. Here we go.

What is Pono?

In a nutshell, Pono is a democratic, outdoor, and urban school, where the children decide their own curriculum. Let's go through this word by word: "Dem-o-crat-ic, adj. Relating to or favoring democracy or its principles" (Merriam-Webster, n.d.). The children,

myself included, are very deeply involved in
what happens at Pono, and every decision is made
together, by consensus. If that's not democracy, I don't
know what is. "Out-door, adj. Done, situated, or used out
of doors; in or into the open-air" (Merriam-Webster,
n.d.). One of my favorite parts of Pono is that we go on a
trip twice a week. It's something I look forward to all
week, and it is always something exciting. People always
ask me which Pono trip was my favorite, but I've been
here for years, so I usually pick one from the previous
week. Child memory loss is real, people!

"Ur-ban, adj. In, relating to, or characteristic of a
town or city" (Merriam- Webster, n.d.). If you look at a
lot of schools that have models similar to Pono's,
you'll probably notice that a lot of them are in some kind
of a forest, or on a farm. Even though I see the appeal of
a school deep in the woods, Pono operates in the
city, because just walking around New York is an
adventure. There are so many interesting places, so many
people with so many stories, and who needs a clear sky
when you have the sky on the ceiling in Grand Central?

I matter!

One of the many ways Pono is child-centered is
in its planning process. Every term, a few weeks before
the break, the children and the adults team up to
create the planning task force we call "The Incredibles."
Oh shoot, that name is taken already, isn't it? Ok, then
let's just say the name is TBD. We all sit down, go
through all of the interests for next term, and see which
ones can work with our budget. This is one of our

biggest differences from other schools, since most schools completely keep their planning process from their students. To be honest, it also helps the teachers, because as any teacher knows, planning is something you need all hands on deck for.

Another thing that is a great example of how important being child-centered is to Pono is council meetings. Whenever a child thinks another is being mean or unkind, the teachers and all the children sit down to talk about it and resolve any issues between the two. This meeting is almost always called by the children, and it is mandatory that everyone attends.

My favorite thing about how child-centered Pono is is how much focus is on each individual child. It's always a nice feeling to know that you are remembered by your teachers, and it's especially helpful while studying a subject that is not your strong suit. This is also helped by the size of the classes. There are 20 students total in Pono, and my class usually has only seven students. Since it's far easier to be overlooked or ignored in a huge class, having a smaller class makes it easy for every child to be given equal attention by the teachers.

One of the things I love most about Pono is how much the opinion of every child matters. How nice is it to feel like you matter, to feel that what you have to say is important, and that your feelings are important too? To me, it's empowering and comforting. One of the pillars of Pono is making every child feel like that, all the time. One example is the planning process I mentioned earlier. There is a rule that every child must have at least 70% of their interests for next term happen, so that not only does everyone get the same amount of control over what happens next term, everyone gets their say.

One of the things I get most annoyed about in Pono is the council meetings. Even though I truly appreciate the idea behind it, it gets very irritating, because when one is called, the entire day stops in its tracks. I'm still smarting from the time we had a council meeting that made me and my friend 45 minutes late for our after-school class. We were not a part of what this meeting was being called about, and hadn't even seen what was going on, but we still had to be there for the whole meeting. Also, there is no real limit to how many you can have per week.

This normally wouldn't bother me, but years ago, we had a child who was going to Pono with his younger brother. Their dynamic was full of taunts and unkind behavior, as is to be expected with many siblings, which caused there to be a council meeting every day of the week. Though there was a change in the interactions between the brothers, it did feel like overkill. If I had to choose any policy in Pono that needs a bit of tweaking, it would be council meetings, without a doubt.

One of the moments in a regular school day where I am reminded very forcibly of how different Pono is from other schools is when we run into them at the playground. The kids from other schools sprint and get kind of violent and scream bloody murder, and there have been multiple times when I've seen a child go off to the side to cry. Not saying the Pono kids can't get a little crazy in the playground (There's been yelping, there's been loose teeth falling out, there's been

screaming of random Russian words—Just don't ask),
but if both classes were guests at the
playground Club, Pono would be the group that's
definitely having a good time, but are not immune to the
appeal of a peaceful seat off to the side, sucking a lemon
wedge.

But the whole reason I'm bringing this up is that
how wild those kids act comes from how little they move
all day. Think about it: They're sitting all day at
their desks, inside all day. They have to get their energy
out somehow lest they lose all feeling in their limbs. And
I think, since we are outside for the better part of
the week and do not have desks, Pono kids are calmer.
And for some reason, whenever I think about that fact, a
wave of peace washes over me, and I am really grateful
that I'm going to this tiny little school—despite the
incredibly loud training group that practices sometimes
out on the street, how the heaters smell like burning hair
when they first get turned on at the beginning of winter,
and the need for the adults to tell random people
repeatedly to not smoke in front of our door—I really
couldn't have asked for anything better.

It was really nice talking to you, but if you don't
mind, I really must get back to my book, because the
Harry Potter series won't reread itself.

References:

Merriam-Webster. (n.d.). Democratic. In *Merriam-
Webster.com dictionary*. Retrieved February 24,
2020 from http://www.merriam-
webster.com/dictionary/citation.

Merriam-Webster. (n.d.). Outdoor. In *Merriam Webster.com dictionary*. Retrieved February 24, 2020 from http://www.merriamwebster.com/dictionary/citation.

Merriam-Webster. (n.d.). Urban. In *Merriam-Webster.com dictionary*. Retrieved February 24, 2020 from http://www.merriam-webster.com/dictionary/citation

Sulaf Hatab is a 12-year-old student at *Pono,* NYCs only democratic, outdoor, urban educational program. She loves rock music, movies, baking, writing, and chocolate in every way, shape, and form.

Chapter 13

The World Is My Classroom

Miro Siegel

Having spent over half of my life traveling abroad, learning from the world around me has become second nature. Through this environment of immersive learning, I have become compassionate, thoughtful, worldly. My perspective has widened and my understanding has deepened. This is what Worldschooling does to a young person.

My name is Miro and I've been a Worldschooler for over 10 years. Having left the United States behind in 2009, I've since been traveling the world with my mom, Lainie. Now, at the time of writing, I am a week away from turning 21, a number with somewhat mythical qualities back where I come from. By the definition of most Americans, I am only just now becoming an adult; a person with real responsibilities, real life experiences, and real opinions. I am to be taken seriously on completing my 21st rotation around the sun, and not a moment sooner.

This cultural ageism is antithetical to everything I've experienced as a Worldschooler growing up. It's contradictory to Worldschooling itself, a learning philosophy that takes strength in exposing learners to new ideas and perspectives, and in granting them the autonomy to follow a path of their own choosing. On a conventional educational path, these are luxuries that are only afforded to learners once they've endured the predetermined curriculum, but I digress.

Through Worldschooling I've had opportunities to make impactful decisions for myself, I've been able to self-actualize and cultivate my own opinions and perspectives. I assume that this is what it feels like to be an adult, but perhaps I'm getting ahead of myself.

Before I go any further, let me give you a clear definition of what Worldschooling is, so that you can better understand my experience. Worldschooling is the immersive, intentional act of learning from the world around you, using the new experiences that travel often presents as a vehicle for deeper exploration. Learning becomes personal, engaging, and hands on, and on top of the rich opportunities for knowledge and skill acquisition, the process itself becomes cultural, emotional and holistic.

This has been my education for the better part of my life. During this time, I've never followed a curriculum, focusing instead on the organic experiences I'd had and the self-directed learning that resulted from them. When we first left the US we carried workbooks in our backpack, less because we actually had the intention of using them and more so because we were told that they were a necessity. Needless to say, within the first few months of our travels our backpacks got much lighter.

My experience with Worldschooling contrasts greatly with the schooling I endured before I left the US. In Los Angeles, I attended a public school where, for 10 hours a day I surrendered my autonomy in exchange for an "education." I was to receive this education in bite-sized, 45-minutes-a-day modules, with the idea that by the time my processing was finished, I'd have exactly one whole body of knowledge, nothing more, nothing less.

As Alfie Kohn put it,

> In a word, learning is decontextualized. We break ideas down into tiny pieces that bear no relation to the whole. We give students a brick of information, followed by another brick, followed by another brick, until they are graduated, at which point we assume they have a house. What they have is a pile of bricks, and they don't have it for long. (2019)

This idea of an approved, complete education was enforced rather strictly at my school, where I was punished for pursuing extracurricular topics and materials, and attempting to take ownership over my own learning process, and learning at my own pace was a crime. I was essentially told that I could only learn within the confines of that classroom. This led me to associate "learning" with my school and my school alone.

In addition to this, learning (now conflated with schooling) was one of the factors that kept me from having a connected relationship with my mom. Once work and school had been accounted for, there was no time for anything other than the essentials.

All of these circumstances led me to my final conclusion: I had decided that I dreaded learning, and began to actively resist it.

When the opportunity to leave everything behind and travel with my mom surfaced, I leapt at it faster than

I've ever leapt at something in my life. It was the first significant decision I'd ever made, and I said yes with every fiber of my being.

Once we started worldschooling, however, I had to unlearn the idea that I hated learning and detox from all of the behaviors I had learned in school. On the road, I began deschooling and started the long and challenging process of adjusting to the new situation I found myself in.

Suddenly, I had an abundance of time, both with myself and with my mom. My voice actually had power now, and I was able to make more decisions for myself. I had the freedom to pursue the things that interested me.

For the first few years, all of these positive changes actually proved to be difficult challenges. Yes, I had time and freedom, but my curiosity and drive to learn hadn't fully recovered yet. For the first time in my life, I was granted autonomy to make decisions, so naturally I acted on impulse as I lacked experience. At first my mom and I clashed, as neither one of us was accustomed to sharing space with the other.

But as time went on, I adapted and adjusted. Each and every one of these points served as a valuable lesson in self-awareness and accountability. I was able to experience natural consequences and was given a safe space to make mistakes, a space which unfortunately isn't available for most people. I learned to take ownership over my actions and responsibility for my shortcomings. And through all of this, I was supported (thanks mom.)

Worldschooling has also affected the way I socialize. Back at my school in LA, my social life was dominated by necessity. Aside from age and geography, what did I have in common with my classmates? I simply went along to get along, and lacked any sense of real connection with them.

Now, my social life is determined by intentionality. The people in my orbit do not share the same physical space, age or background, yet they are still an integral part of my life. I have learned to be in relationships because I want to be in them, not just because I can be. I have chosen my people and they have chosen me.

Learning doesn't just stop when you hit a certain age, it's a lifelong process and now, as I am on the cusp of adulthood, I am still Worldschooling. If anything, Worldschooling has best taught me how to learn; I don't break my learning down into subjects, I learn at my own pace, I find myself constantly learning and, most importantly, I enjoy learning.

I still have so much to learn, and what a joyful thing that is.

References

Kohn, A. (2019). Punished by rewards: The trouble with gold stars, incentive plans, A's, praise, and other bribes. New York: Houghton, Mifflin and Company.

Miro Siegel is a 23-year-old traveler and youth facilitator for Project World School. His learning is self-directed and influenced by the ever-changing world around him. To him, this is Worldschooling. He is interested in, and is an advocate for children's rights, travel as education and a spearhead of the Worldschooling movement that he and his mother helped create. Miro Siegel traveled to Amsterdam in April, 2016 to present at the TEDxAmsterdamED conference and to bring a slightly more "unconventional" view to the table. In 2017, Miro attended the Youth Global Changemakers Summit in Switzerland, one of 60 delegates selected from over 6,000 applicants. He aspires to bring cultural awareness and immersion to more people, because he truly believes that travel can bring peace to the world and inspire learning without measure.

Chapter 14

Summerhill

Jasmine Higgins

Summerhill was my whole world for the first 18 years of my life. To say how it has impacted me is tricky, like trying to describe how it feels to be left-handed: I may be aware that it's a bit different, but it's the only thing that makes sense to me. The founder of Summerhill, A.S. Neill, was my great-grandfather. My grandma, mum, and uncles all attended the school, so it only made sense that I would go there too.

When I was about 4 and just beginning to attend school for a few hours a day, I didn't like it. I wanted to be at home where all my things were. I remember telling my mum I didn't want to go, and she told me that if I wasn't at Summerhill, I'd have to go to a normal school where I'd have to do as I was told.

This concept shocked me. I knew from an early age that I deserved the trust and respect of those around me, adults and kids alike, to spend my own time how I wanted. I didn't complain about school again.

Instead, I started to explore what I could do in this new environment. Instead of crying under a chair until my mum came to pick me up, I'd run around outside and climb trees. In class, I'd often spend time with my teachers instead of friends since I enjoyed adult company. They never made me feel annoying or unwelcome; I felt like I could be anyone's friend regardless of age or status.

My younger brother started school 2 years after me, and I attempted to look after him, but he quickly

Jasmine Higgins

made friends and didn't want me hanging around him all the time. As a protective older sibling, I had to learn to give him space at school.

The San

The youngest age group in Summerhill is called "the San." San kids, aged 5-8, have their own area that consists of living accommodation, a sandpit, Class 1, the San swings, and San field. There is also a climbing structure and a trampoline in this area. The bedrooms are a mix of girls and boys.

Children from older age groups are allowed in the San area, although San kids can ask them to leave. It's a safe space for the youngest kids in the school, and in my time, we would get a bit territorial and enjoyed using our power to keep the area to ourselves.

Of all the age groups, the San feels the most like a bubble, where you mainly spend time around kids your own age. However, we did enjoy winding up the big kids so they'd chase us, and we would be around them a lot at mealtimes, meetings, etc.

Class 1

San kids are taught in Class 1. Class 1 ranges from roughly age 4-9, and most subjects are taught in the same building, with some exceptions such as Woodwork that requires a specific space and tools.

In Class 1, I remember having History lessons and building the Great Fire of London out of card. We also had regular Story Time where we read things like

Chapter 14

Roald Dahl and *The Chronicles of Narnia*. I remember
growing watercress in Science and teaching my friends
how to draw horses. I remember counting and colour-
grouping sweets in Maths, and the empowerment I felt
from learning to read. At this age, we also spent a lot of
time playing outside. Finding the perfect stick to claim
as a sword, building dens in the woods, and climbing lots
of trees.

School Meetings

At the core of Summerhill is the school meeting,
where rules are made and issues are discussed. Everyone
has an equal vote, regardless of age.

Younger children are often less involved in
school meetings, although the option to participate is
always there if they want it. I think when you're older,
you feel more of a responsibility to know what's going
on so you can look after your school, but when you're
little you don't have as much patience in meetings unless
the case directly concerns you.

My friends and I tended not to attend meetings, at
least not for the full duration, when we were in the San.
We would go if we had our own cases to bring up—if
the trampoline rule was that 3 San kids could go on at
once, but we wanted to go on as a group of 4, we would
need to propose an exception.

The meeting can feel very liberating as you start
to learn the power it holds. Small disputes, such as
name-calling, tend to be resolved by an Ombudsman (a
Shack or Carriage kid who has been elected), however,
sometimes children will prefer to bring these things to

the meeting. In the case of San kids, it's often their way of dipping their toes in and learning about the meeting. The realisation of *"I didn't like what you did/said, and I can bring you up for it!"* is an empowering Summerhill experience that all young or new pupils have.

I got brought up for the first time when I was about 8. My brother and I had stayed a night at school, and as we weren't regular boarders yet, this was very exciting for us and our roommates. We woke up early, probably around 7 a.m., and decided to get up and go to play in the woods behind the San. Summerhill has "silence hour" which means you must be quiet while people are sleeping—this is between your bedtime (San bedtime is around 9 p.m.) until "wake-up" which is 8 a.m. for the whole school.

We were up making noise before 8 a.m., which woke up our houseparent. She decided to bring us up in the meeting for breaking silence hour, and proposed we get a strong warning not to do it again. It felt quite daunting, hearing my own name in a case where I had done something wrong, and watching people vote on what fine I should receive. It was a quick and easy case, and the strong warning got carried. I understood what I had done wrong and that it had negatively affected someone else.

I was never one to get in lots of trouble; I was the type to follow rules carefully and avoid conflict. The meeting always listened and respected people, and I felt a strong sense of wanting to give that same respect back to them. I was never afraid of punishment when getting brought up—I didn't need to be punished to care about what I had done. Having an open discussion with the community was enough to understand the impact of my actions, and I didn't want to take the school's patience for granted.

The Cottage

When I was 9, I moved up to the second age group known as "the Cottage." The main differences were a later bedtime and segregated rooms—I had mostly been friends with boys, so it was a bit of a change sharing a room with only girls.

Class 2

This also moved me up into Class 2. Class 2 has a free space for general projects such as arts & crafts, a room where lessons take place, and a library. I rarely went to lessons in Class 2, but I spent every day in there drawing, making, and chatting with friends. Some days I would work on my own, and other days we might work as a group on projects we'd come up with together. In the summer, we would make things for Half Term Sale—a fundraising event for the school that is attended by families and ex-pupils. I remember making coasters, bookmarks, and lavender cushions. We would then run a stall at the Sale. I hadn't been to a maths lesson for years at this point, but I felt happy and confident giving people their change and counting our money after the sale, despite my lack of classroom-based learning.

As technology was rapidly advancing throughout my childhood, there were often changes to screening rules as the Summerhill community tried to figure out what to do about gaming. When I was a Cottage kid, there were no screening rules for a while, meaning I could play on my Nintendo DS all day if I wanted. There were definitely days where this was the case, but Class 2 acted as a nice escape as it was such a lovely social space. I can't remember if we were allowed to go on screens in classrooms or not, but I never took my DS to play in there.

I think the screening rules still change from time to time, but the rule is usually that you can't go on social media, watch TV, or play computer games until after lessons end at around 3 p.m. I much preferred this over having no screening rules as kids play outside more when they can't go on screens, and older kids who tend to go to more lessons are usually social between their classes as well. This is one of many things that might sound like it's decided by adults, but as always, everyone votes and there are enough people of all ages who prefer to have some limits with screen time.

During my time in the Cottage, there were some issues among my roommates. There were 5 of us sharing a room, and one girl we found difficult to get along with. At first, we were just fed up with her being loud and messy, but it escalated, and we would call her names and play tricks on her. In my case, I got along with her individually, but there were issues between her and my close friends, so I found myself on their "side."

The school meeting got quite frustrated with us. At every meeting, she would try to bring us up for something silly, and we'd do the same to her. Everyone was tired of hearing us back and forth, trying to "win" by getting the other in trouble. We were going against what meetings are there for. We knew we were doing it, too, but we'd try to insist that we were genuinely upset by the trivial things we would bring to the meeting.

Everyone saw right through this. The issue was never that she slammed the door too loudly or we called her a name—it was that we didn't get along. We were nit-picking because "I just don't like her" didn't feel like a valid meeting case.

Eventually, there was a general case about us as a room. It's rare for this to happen—I maybe saw it 2-3 times in my years at Summerhill—and it was a very different feeling to all the other cases where it was me on one side and her on the other. In this case, we were all the problem, and we were all the solution. It was carried that we would get a Room Ombudsman. This would be someone experienced on the Ombudsman committee, and they would sit down with us and try to talk through what was going on.

Our Ombudsman was a girl aged around 16. She'd helped us resolve issues before, so she volunteered as she was already familiar with us. She got us all together and asked us to write down things we liked and disliked about sharing a room.

This was an unusual occurrence at Summerhill. I rarely saw a situation be moved from the meeting to an Ombudsman case—it usually worked the other way around.

By this point, I was tired from the months of winding each other up, and our room issues had made it harder to go and play with other kids as they were a bit fed up with us too, from sitting through all our meeting cases!

I'd also recently spent some time alone with my roommate. We'd gone to borrow some nature magazines from Class 1, then we sat on the floor cutting out pictures to stick on our walls. We both agreed that we didn't hate each other as much as we thought.

So, when asked to write down something I liked about sharing a room with her, I wrote, "Sometimes we like cutting out pictures together." This seemed to simplify everything as from then on, we were great friends.

There were probably several solutions to our situation, and a Room Ombudsman was just one of them, but this was how things were eventually resolved in our case and I wanted to share it because this was the most "difficult" phase I had at school. Serious bullying is rare, but there are of course mild cases and nastiness from time to time, and I don't think there's really a default solution since all cases are different. Moving forward, I became more patient with kids who were frequently being brought up as I'd been there, and I knew they were capable of change.

The House

I moved up to "the House" when I was 11. This is when I started boarding full-time, so I went from going home every weekend to only going a few times per term. This was a big change, and I did feel homesick from time to time, but my friends and roommates were all so supportive. I felt a lot closer to everyone once I started living at school, since they all lived there together so sometimes as a day kid I would miss out on things in the evenings.

New experiences I got as a full time boarder included movie nights in the café, games in the evening such as "kick the can" and "paper game," and chatting with my roommates after lights out (although we were meant to be sleeping!). I still didn't go to a lot of lessons at this age, but I did the odd History or English lesson, and I attended jewellery workshops that were run by an ex-pupil. I really enjoyed these and they must have stuck with me, as I still make necklaces now and I sell them online as a little side business. I also enjoyed writing little poems and lyrics in my own time.

The House was when I started getting involved with school committees. Some required being in an older age group, and I'll talk about those later, but as a House kid I enjoyed working for Picture Committee. This is a group of people in charge of decorating the Lounge (where meetings usually take place) for our half term and end of term parties. The Lounge closes for a few days and, based on a theme chosen by the committee, the room is transformed with paintings, sculptures, streamers, and balloons. The theme is kept top-secret by the committee and no one else is allowed in the Lounge until the party. Themes can be anything from "underwater" to "Alice in Wonderland," and there's often a lot of excitement about the big reveal—some kids would queue for hours outside the Lounge waiting for the party to start.

I loved being behind the scenes getting everything ready and hoping people would be surprised. It could be quite nerve-wracking to have people looking at my art, but I think this was good practice for the art exhibitions I had to do at university.

The responsibility also felt great. I worked hard on the committee because I knew there would be a lot of hype about the party, and the nuisance of the Lounge being closed had to be worth it for all the people who weren't allowed in. I always kept little scraps after the parties such as paintings or party hats, and I'd write little notes on them detailing which party they were from and who made them. I still like looking at these since I remember the parties so fondly.

The Shack

Moving up to the Shack means a new level of responsibility. You still don't *have* to do things you don't want to, but there are some important committees most of us felt we should be a part of. This is the age group where you start to feel like one of the "big kids."

I moved up to the Shack aged 13, and during my first term in the Shack, I was on both Ombudsman and Beddies Officer committees. These both change every term so that new people have a chance to run.

The Ombudsmen are people you can go to with an issue that doesn't need to go to the meeting. Issues that can be resolved by talking to both sides and figuring out who is in the wrong. If someone calls you a name, the Ombudsman will normally tell them not to do it again, after speaking to them and finding out whether it was provoked or not. Sometimes it is clear that two kids are simply annoyed with each other, and the Ombudsman might suggest they just leave each other alone for a bit. If it seems like more of a meeting case, the Ombudsman might bring up the case on their behalf or tell them to do it themselves.

Beddies Officers are in charge of making sure everyone gets up in the morning and goes to bed at their bedtime. They work in pairs, so every day there are 2 Beddies Officers who do both the morning and evening of that day.

I sometimes found it difficult to assert myself when people didn't follow the rules, but I got better at it over time and having the power to give out fines was great. Wakeup was at 8 a.m., and everyone had to be out of bed by 8:30. I believe the standard fine for sleeping in was 10% of your pocket money (given out weekly), and it was the same for sneaking out after lights-out, although we could give whatever fines we deemed appropriate. If someone felt they had been fined too harshly, they could ask the meeting for an appeal, and as Beddies Officer you would explain why you gave the fine so the meeting could make their decision on the appeal.

Class 3

Shack kids are in Class 3, meaning you no longer have a designated building for most of your classes, but rather you have different classrooms dotted around the school for different subjects. While in Class 1 & 2 there is a teacher who covers many subjects, Class 3 has more teachers who specialise in different areas.

Shack kids are given a Careers Advisor. This is a member of staff who discusses the future with you and

Jasmine Higgins

assists in planning your moves towards leaving school. There is still no pressure from Summerhill or your Careers Advisor to go to lessons or take exams, but at this age, kids usually start to think more realistically.

My interests at the time were music and makeup. I particularly loved nail art and would sometimes paint my nails multiple times a day, trying new designs. I started regularly going to guitar lessons when I was 13, and I was eager to improve as I loved writing lyrics and wanted to start writing my songs on guitar as well.

It was clear that my interests were mostly creative, so it made sense to keep focusing on art and music. I also started going to some Science lessons since I'd read it was required to study Beauty Therapy at college, which I thought I might want to do at the time to potentially become a nail technician.

I eventually found that nails and guitar were an awkward pair of hobbies, since playing guitar would mess up my nails, and I couldn't grow my nails out too long on my left hand since they made it difficult to play. I started to prioritise guitar because it linked with my other passion for songwriting, and I started focusing less on nails and more on general makeup.

When I was 14, I went all in with lessons and started going to Maths, English, History, Geography, Calligraphy, and Singing. It was a little daunting because I feared everyone might know more than I, seeing as other kids my age had been going to lessons for years and had attended normal schools before Summerhill.

I was actually very comfortable in class, and I wasn't behind others by any means. In my first maths lesson, my teacher simply wanted to see how familiar I

230

was with using a calculator. In English, I learned about verbs and adjectives. If I didn't know something, I got comfortable with asking, and no one laughed at me. Everything was paced nicely.

It felt good getting into a routine with lessons. I still skipped lessons when I wanted to, but I liked the feeling of working together with my classmates spending more time around teachers. I knew how fulfilling it must be for them to know the kids in their class are choosing to be there, and although there was still no pressure from anyone else, I felt a sense of purpose within myself to go and be a part of the things I'd signed up for.

The Carriages

I moved up to the Carriages, the oldest age group, when I was 15. This was exciting because it meant getting my own room and having no real bedtime—we just had to be in our rooms/building after midnight. I had some fun with this new freedom, and I had some late nights with friends staying up in my room chatting, but I was determined to keep going to lessons. Freedom is a responsibility and I wanted to use it wisely now that I was older.

I began working towards English, History, and Science GCSEs at 15. The following year, I also began working towards Psychology and Art. This meant I completed 3 GCSEs when I was 17, and 2 more when I was 18.

I wasn't sure what my required grades would be for college. I was still considering a diploma in Beauty Therapy, although I was starting to worry that I wouldn't enjoy the jobs I could get from it. I was also considering a diploma in Art & Design, but I wasn't sure how I'd use that either. Exams felt like a lot of work considering that I hadn't been going to lessons for very long, but the work was very manageable. I can't believe it when I hear people from normal schools talk about taking 9 GCSEs at once—that's extreme!

Our summer terms would finish a bit later than most schools, meaning we had plenty of time after exams to spend outdoors just enjoying the school. The swimming pool opens during the summer, and there are always games and events going on outside.

In my last year, I performed at the end of term music event. This was something I always wanted to do, but shied away from, so it was important to me that I took that last chance to get up on stage. It was scary and imperfect, but I loved it.

My final year, and especially that last summer term, were very emotional for me. I was leaving my home and my family. I couldn't imagine being anywhere else with anyone else—these people were my whole world. I went around revisiting memories from my childhood; climbing trees I used to climb when I was six. I tried to spend time with everyone. I cried so much I felt sick, and it was agonising trying to find the strength to take down my posters, accepting that I was moving out of my room, permanently. At the end of term, I stayed up all night for the party and to say goodbye to international students who got a bus to the airport around 6 a.m. A friend who was also leaving slept through the first bus and couldn't stop crying because he didn't get the chance to say goodbye.

Chapter 14

Leaving Summerhill was extremely heavy for all of us, but it had to be. It was cathartic. This place was such an important chapter in our lives, and it deserved an emotional ending.

After

I moved to Norwich to go to college with my best friend who left Summerhill at the same time as I did. We got a little flat together, and I studied Art & Design after achieving the required grades. Since I didn't take a Maths GCSE, it was required that I studied Maths at college, so I took the classes as needed. In my second year of college, I was no longer required to take Maths. My tutors encouraged me to carry on and take the GCSE in case I wanted to go to university, but I chose to stop. I didn't want any other studies to distract me from art.

Leaving Summerhill, I was afraid that everyone would know more than I did and that I wouldn't fit in as my childhood was so different from everyone else's. I quickly found that, when starting out somewhere new, everyone is afraid they won't fit in. I found a group of friends who loved and accepted me for who I am, despite not always understanding my unconventional background. I realised that I'll meet special people everywhere at different times in my life, and although my Summerhill family is forever and so unique, I can feel at home and understood in other places, too.

At college, I discovered video as an art medium. I ended the first year with a Distinction (A) and decided video was my "thing," so I stuck with it for the whole of my second year. Sometimes I would include writing, such as poetry, in my films.

I decided to apply to university for the sole reason of knowing I didn't have to go just because I had applied. However, I quickly found myself excited by the places I visited on open days and the offers I was receiving. I made the decision to move to London and study Fine Art at Kingston University.

My Fine Art course involved mostly independent, self-directed learning. I think most people assume this kind of course is ideal for an ex-Summerhillian, but I found myself quite frustrated at times. I was there to learn! University is expensive, and I was paying to mess around and do what I wanted. This freedom was ground-breaking and liberating for many of my classmates, but I'd got that out of my system already and I wanted to be challenged.

Still, I enjoyed the course, and I used my flexible schedule to work on lots of things I loved. In the summer of first year, I wrote a draft of a novel I still intend to finish. Then, the summer of second year, I wrote a collection of poetry which I self-published during third year. I submitted this as part of my coursework and finished my degree with a First.

I found through my art studies that, although video is something I find very satisfying to work with, I don't see myself as a "filmmaker." I do, however, feel like a writer. It's always been there, whether in the form of lyrics or poetry or unfinished novels.

I moved back home during lockdown in 2020, and I had the chance to briefly work at Summerhill as a cleaner. One of my favourite things about all age groups being together in one place is that, since I only left a few years ago, the little kids from my time are still there, and they're now the big kids. They remember me from when they were in the San, and I'd tuck them into bed as Beddies Officer. My little cousins are also at Summerhill now and seeing them at school playing is just so special.

I'm now starting an MA in Publishing. I decided I'd rather learn about the industry I'm interested in, instead of continuing to use my art and writing for grades. I think creativity is nurtured rather than taught, and from now on, I want to do that in my own time. I'm excited to be on a course that feels more practical and informative.

I can't speak on what I'll end up doing for a living, but I can say I'm endlessly grateful for growing up in an environment that supported me as a creative person. I feel so lucky to be a writer and artist. Being hardly employable is a challenge I rather enjoy; people told me I couldn't go to university without Maths, and I did it anyway. People told me art must be visual, so I wrote a book instead of painting portraits for my degree. People told me you can't get anywhere with an art qualification, so I used my art degree to get onto a different degree. I get little thrills from finding loopholes in the system, and I suspect I'll someday find myself in a job that requires more maths than I can handle. If that happens, I'll happily take that Maths GCSE. I'd happily do it if I could see a purpose for it, but so far, I just don't. I only commit myself to things that matter to me.

I don't know quite what I'll end up doing, but I hope that somewhere down the line I end up back at

Jasmine Higgins

Summerhill, giving back to the place that gave me
everything.

Jasmine Higgins attended Summerhill from 2001-2005.
She is the great grandchild of A.S. Neill. She is a poet
and hopeful future novelist based in London. She has a
BA in Fine Art and an MA in Publishing, both from
Kingston University. Her first book *A Girl is a
Shapeshifter* came out in 2019, and her second book
Mermaid Lungs came out in 2022.

www.ingramcontent.com/pod-product-compliance
Lightning Source LLC
Chambersburg PA
CBHW071604030726
47593CB00001BA/306